- INSTALL ELECTRICAL BREAKERS FOR ENTIRE SHOP WITHIN EASY REACH, CIRCUIT-RATED FOR SUFFICIENT AMPERAGE
- STOCK FIRST AID KIT WITH MATERIALS TO TREAT CUTS, GASHES, SPLINTERS, FOREIGN OBJECTS AND CHEMICALS IN EYES, AND BURNS
- HAVE TELEPHONE IN SHOP TO CALL FOR HELP
- INSTALL FIRE EXTINGUISHER RATED FOR A-, B-, AND C-CLASS FIRES
- WEAR EYE PROTECTION AT ALL TIMES
- LOCK CABINETS AND POWER TOOLS TO PROTECT CHILDREN AND INEXPERIENCED VISITORS
- USE DUST COLLECTOR TO KEEP SHOP DUST AT A MINIMUM
- WEAR SHIRT SLEEVES ABOVE ELBOWS
- WEAR CLOSE-FITTING CLOTHES
- WEAR LONG PANTS
- REMOVE WATCHES, RINGS, OR JEWELRY
- KEEP TABLE AND FENCE SURFACES WAXED AND RUST-FREE
- WEAR THICK-SOLED SHOES, PREFERABLY WITH STEEL TOES

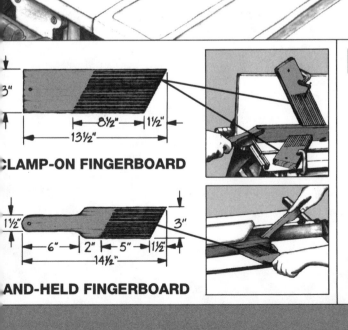

3"

8½" — 1½"

13½"

CLAMP-ON FINGERBOARD

1½"

3"

6" — 2" — 5" — 1½"

14½"

HAND-HELD FINGERBOARD

PROTECTION

WEAR FULL FACE SHIELD DURING LATHE TURNING, ROUTING, AND OTHER OPERATIONS THAT MAY THROW CHIPS

WEAR DUST MASK DURING SANDING AND SAWING

WEAR VAPOR MASK DURING FINISHING

WEAR SAFETY GLASSES OR GOGGLES AT ALL TIMES

WEAR RUBBER GLOVES FOR HANDLING DANGEROUS CHEMICALS

WEAR EAR PROTECTORS DURING ROUTING, PLANING, AND LONG, CONTINUOUS POWER TOOL OPERATION

THE WORKSHOP COMPANION™

USING THE SCROLL SAW

TECHNIQUES FOR BETTER WOODWORKING

by Nick Engler

Rodale Press
Emmaus, Pennsylvania

Printed in the United States of America on acid-free ∞,
recycled ♲ paper

If you have any questions or comments concerning this
book, please write:
 Rodale Press
 Book Readers' Service
 33 East Minor Street
 Emmaus, PA 18098

About the Author: Nick Engler is an experienced wood-
worker, writer, and teacher. He worked as a luthier for
many years, making traditional American musical instru-
ments before he founded *Hands On!* magazine. Today, he
contributes to several woodworking magazines and teaches
woodworking at the University of Cincinnati. He has written
more than three dozen books.

Series Editor: Bob Moran
Editor: Roger Yepsen
Copy Editor: Barbara Webb
Graphic Designer: Linda Watts
Illustrator: Mary Jane Favorite
Master Craftsman: Jim McCann
Photographer: Karen Callahan
Cover Photographer: Mitch Mandel
Proofreader: Hue Park
Indexer: Beverly Bremer
Typesetting by Computer Typography, Huber Heights, Ohio
Interior and endpaper illustrations by Mary Jane Favorite
Produced by Bookworks, Inc., West Milton, Ohio

Library of Congress Cataloging-in-Publication Data

Engler, Nick.
 Using the scroll saw/by Nick Engler.
  p.   cm. — (The workshop companion)
 Includes index.
 ISBN 0–87596–654–3 hardcover
 1. Jig saws. 2. Woodwork. I. Title II. Series:
Engler, Nick. Workshop companion.
TT186.E527 1994
684'.083—dc20   94–14418
                                              CIP

2 4 6 8 10 9 7 5 3   hardcover

Special Thanks to:

Delta International Machinery
Corporation
Pittsburgh, Pennsylvania

Jim Berkley
Shopsmith, Inc.
Dayton, Ohio

Chuck Olson
The Olson Saw Company
Bethel, Connecticut

Ray Seymore
Seyco
Garland, Texas

The Tool Company, Inc.
Raymore, Missouri

George F. Vander Voort
Carpenter Technology Corporation
Reading, Pennslyvania

Wertz Hardware
West Milton, Ohio

CONTENTS

TECHNIQUES

PROJECTS

TECHNIQUES

1

CHOOSING A SCROLL SAW

The evolution of the scroll saw is linked to the rise in popularity of *fretwork* — the sawing of intricate shapes from wood. Although there are examples of fretwork-like decorations on early Egyptian, Greek, and Roman furniture, these were probably carved or cut with a knife. It wasn't possible to saw delicate wooden shapes until the late 1500s, when a German craftsman (possibly a clock maker) devised a method for making fine, narrow blades.

About a century later, Andre Charles Boulle of Paris developed many of the basic techniques for fretwork, as well as marquetry and inlay (which also involve sawing complex shapes). He also invented several tools for this work, including the U-shaped *fret saw,* originally known as the *Buhl-saw* (Buhl being a corruption of his name). Boulle's work established fretwork as a craft in its own right and popularized it throughout Europe. Fretwork became especially fashionable in Italy — within a generation of Boulle's death, many of the recognized masters were working in and around Sorrento. In fact, fretwork was introduced into America in the mid-1800s as *Sorrento wood carving.*

The craft caught on swiftly in this country, as evidenced by the vast amounts of fretwork in American architecture and furniture from the period. However, Americans apparently were *not* particularly enamored with the tedious handwork required to produce it. By the 1860s, the first mechanical fret saws — called *scroll saws* — began to appear in the United States.

The earliest scroll saws married the hand-held fret saw to another cutting tool that had been around for a few centuries: the reciprocating saw or *sash saw.* Old-time craftsmen mounted a saw blade in a sash (frame), then attached the top of the sash to a supple pole and the bottom to a foot treadle. Stepping on the treadle pulled the saw down through a worktable, cutting the stock that rested there. When the pressure was released, the pole pulled the saw up again, readying it for the next stroke. By substituting a narrow fret blade for the wider sash blade, toolmakers created a stationary tool for fretwork. Over the next 75 years, hundreds of scroll saw models appeared on the market, powered by foot treadles, water, steam, electric motors, even pedals like those on a bicycle.

In the 1930s, the demand for fretwork temporarily waned. Tastes in architecture and furniture were more austere; fretwork was considered an excess rather than a decoration. The evolution of the scroll saw slowed to a crawl until the 1970s, when a new interest in handcrafts revived the old art form. With demand once again on the increase, manufacturers took a new look at the tool and introduced machines engineered for better balance, smoother cuts, and easier operation. Today there are well over fifty models of scroll saws available, offering many different features and capacities.

2

SCROLL SAW FEATURES

WHAT A SCROLL SAW DOES

A scroll saw is used almost exclusively for creating fine, complex shapes and patterns such as fretwork, marquetry, intarsia, and inlay. The machine mounts a narrow, delicate blade, suspending it vertically in a frame. The frame and the blade *reciprocate* — move up and down as the saw cuts. Different blades are used to cut wood, metals, and other materials.

You can use a scroll saw to cut both *exterior* and *interior* shapes. To make an exterior shape, simply cut around the perimeter or outside edge. To make an interior shape, drill a hole in the workpiece, thread the blade through the hole, and start sawing. By starting in the center of the stock, you can cut out the inside of a pattern without slicing through the stock from the outside edge.

Scroll saws make very smooth cuts. The blades have more teeth per inch than other sawing tools, the teeth are finer, and they usually have no set. Consequently, the saw marks are almost undetectable. The sawed surfaces require little sanding — another reason why a scroll saw is the best power tool for making elaborate shapes and patterns.

FOR YOUR INFORMATION

Because scroll saw blades have such fine teeth and cut slowly, they are generally much safer than other sawing tools. For this reason, the scroll saw is a good machine on which to teach woodworking to children.

TYPES OF SCROLL SAWS

Scroll saws differ widely in their design and capacities, but all have a few important features in common. The *blade* extends through a *worktable* and is held in place by two *arms* that pivot up and down. *Blade clamps* attach the blade to the arms and make it possible to change blades easily. Tightening the *tension adjustment* makes the blade taut and keeps it rigid as it cuts. (*SEE FIGURE 1-1.*) On a few machines, the blade is tensioned by a spring and held by a single stationary arm. On all machines, a *motor* turns an *eccentric*, which drives a *pitman arm*. The eccentric and the pitman convert the rotary motion of the motor into linear (reciprocating) motion and drive the blade up and down.

1-1 On a typical scroll saw, the *blade* (1) extends through the **work-table** (2) and is attached to the front ends of an **upper arm** (3) and **lower arm** (4) by **blade clamps** (5). A **tensioning rod** (6) connects the arms at the back ends. When you tighten the **tension adjustment** (7) at the top of the rod, the blade becomes taut. The arms are mounted on **pivots** (8) in a **frame** (9). The lower arm is connected to a **motor** (10) by a **pitman arm** (11) and an **eccentric** (12). The motor turns the eccentric, which drives the pitman arm up and down. This, in turn, drives the lower arm and all the parts that are linked to it, including the blade. The worktable is mounted on a **trunnion** (13) so that it can be tilted. A **hold-down** (14) keeps the work firmly against the worktable as you cut. A **blower** (15) directs a stream of air where the blade meets the workpiece to clear sawdust away from the pattern lines. The blower, worktable, frame, and

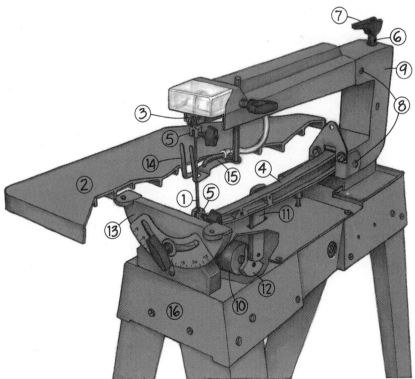

motor are all mounted to a *base* (16). **Note:** Not all scroll saws have every feature listed, but all work on the

same principle: They hold a fine blade under tension and drive it up and down to make a cut.

Scroll saws are categorized according to the mechanism used to move the blade up and down. Currently, there are four distinct types (*SEE FIGURE 1-2*):

■ The *parallel-arm* scroll saw (sometimes called a *walking beam* saw) is the most common type. It has two long arms mounted on pivots. The arms are linked at the front end by the blade and at the back end by a tension rod, forming a flexible parallelogram. (*SEE FIGURE 1-3.*) The advantage of this arrangement is that as the arms rock up and down, the blade remains absolutely vertical in the cut. This makes it easier to turn tight corners and make precision cuts.

■ On a *double-parallel link* scroll saw, the arms are linked to small levers that hold the blade. They don't pivot, but slide horizontally. As they move back and forth, they push and pull on the levers, which drive the blade up and down. As with the parallel-arm saw, the blade remains vertical in the cut. (*SEE FIGURE 1-4.*) The advantage of this system is that, theoretically, it creates less vibration. Because the arms move in opposite directions, their inertial forces cancel each other out.

■ In a *C-frame* scroll saw, the blade is held in a rigid C-shaped frame, and the entire frame is

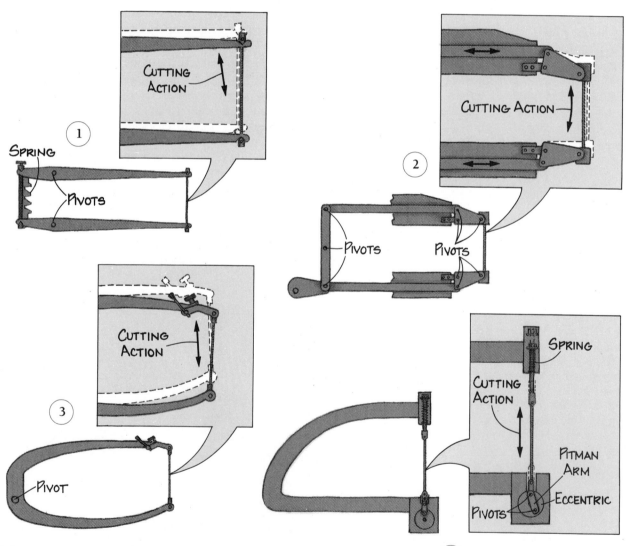

1-2 Four types of mechanism are used to move a scroll saw blade up and down — *parallel-arm* (1), *double-parallel link* (2), *C-frame* (3), and *rigid-arm* (4). The first three are *constant-tension* systems because the blade remains at the same tension throughout each stroke. In the last system — the rigid-arm — the blade tension is always changing.

mounted on a single pivot. Because of this, the blade moves in an arc — it doesn't remain straight up and down in the cut. Furthermore, as the massive frame rocks up and down, it generates strong vibrations. (*SEE FIGURE 1-5.*) This arrangement will cut reasonably well if the vibration is properly damped, but it's not the best for tight curves, sharp corners, or precision cutting.

■ On a *rigid-arm* scroll saw (better known as a *jigsaw*), the arm doesn't move at all. Instead, a powerful spring mounted on the end of the arm holds the top of the blade, and the bottom is attached to the pitman arm. As the eccentric rotates, the blade is alternately pulled down by the pitman and up by the spring. (*SEE*

FIGURE 1-6.) Although there are fewer moving parts in this mechanism, it's hard on the blades. The blade tension is not constant — it increases during the downstroke and decreases on the way up. Blades break more often and sometimes bow in the cut.

Scroll saws are available in both *bench* models (without a stand) and *stationary* models. (*SEE FIGURE 1-7.*) Bench models are less expensive and, in some cases, more flexible than stationary machines — you can build your own stand, placing the saw at a comfortable working height. You can also add storage to the stand to hold scroll saw blades and accessories. (For plans and instructions on how to build a stand, see the "Scroll Saw Storage Stand" on page 93.)

1-3 Most scroll saws are parallel-arm or "walking beam" saws, such as the RBI saw shown. Both arms pivot independently, keeping the blade under constant tension and straight up and down in the cut. The major problem with this arrangement is vibration. The moving parts — the arms, in particular — must be as light as possible to keep the vibration at a minimum, while the other parts must be as massive as possible to dampen the vibration.

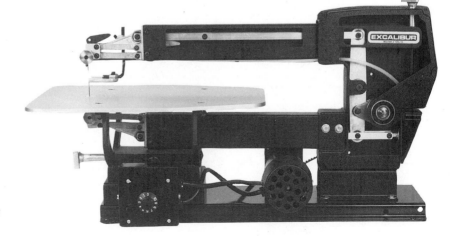

1-4 Excalibur saw models EX-19 and EX-30 use a unique double-parallel link mechanism. As with a parallel-arm saw, the blade remains under constant tension and perfectly vertical. Theoretically, this design produces less vibration because the inertial forces generated by the moving parts are more evenly balanced than in other systems. In practice, however, these machines seem to vibrate just as much as a well-made parallel-arm scroll saw. *Photo courtesy of Seyco.*

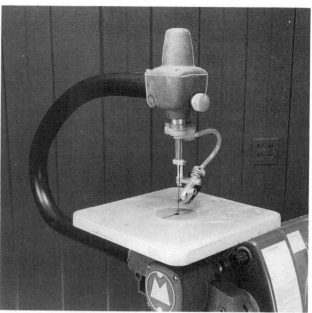

1-5 The C-frame is the simplest
of the scroll saw mechanical systems
— the frame rocks on a single pivot.
This design keeps the blade at a
constant tension, but the blade
travels in a small arc and does not
remain vertical in the cut. Furthermore, the C-frame tends to generate
stronger vibrations than other designs.
Only a few manufacturers make
C-frame saws; the model shown is
a Delta. *Photo courtesy of Delta
International Machinery Corporation.*

1-6 A jigsaw, such as this older
Shopsmith, is a scroll saw with a
rigid arm. The arm does not pivot;
instead, the blade is attached to a
spring so it can move up and down.
This keeps the blade vertical in the
cut, and because the moving parts
aren't as massive as those on other
systems, vibration is not as big a
problem. However, there are more
problems with blade tension — it
increases and decreases with each
stroke. This, in turn, puts a lot of
wear and tear on the blade.

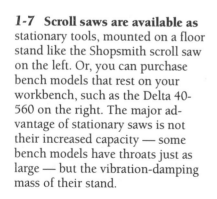

1-7 Scroll saws are available as
stationary tools, mounted on a floor
stand like the Shopsmith scroll saw
on the left. Or, you can purchase
bench models that rest on your
workbench, such as the Delta 40-
560 on the right. The major advantage of stationary saws is not
their increased capacity — some
bench models have throats just as
large — but the vibration-damping
mass of their stand.

CAPACITIES AND SPEEDS

Scroll saws are also classified by their *throat capacity* — the distance from the blade to the frame. (*See Figure 1-8.*) The capacities of most machines range from 12 to 30 inches. This determines how large a workpiece may be cut. If you have a 15-inch scroll saw, the throat capacity of the machine is 15 inches, enabling you to saw to the middle of a 30-inch-diameter pattern.

A scroll saw also has a *thickness capacity*. (*Again, see Figure 1-8.*) The distance from the worktable to the upper blade clamp at the lowest point in the stroke determines the thickest possible workpiece you can cut. For most saws, this is a little over 2 inches. It really isn't practical to cut anything thicker than that even if you have the capacity; the blade is not rigid enough. Besides, the thicker the workpiece, the longer it takes to cut.

The cutting speed of a scroll saw is measured in *strokes per minute* (spm). Some machines have more than one speed; others are electrically or mechanically variable. Most one-speed saws cut between 1,200 and 1,800 spm, while a variable-speed saw may range from 400 to 1,800 spm. The higher end of the speed range is used mostly for cutting wood and plywood; lower speeds are useful for cutting veneers, metals, plastic, bone, and similar materials.

The length of each stroke — the vertical distance the blade moves — is an important specification. With a longer stroke, more teeth engage the wood; the blade clears the sawdust better, remains cooler, and stays sharp longer. But if the stroke is *too* long, the saw may vibrate excessively. The stroke length on most saws will be between $\frac{5}{8}$ and $1\frac{1}{4}$ inches. (*See Figure 1-9.*)

1-8 The throat capacity of a scroll saw — the distance from the blade to the frame — determines the *largest* workpiece you can cut. The thickness capacity — the distance from the table to the blade clamp at the lowest point in the stroke — determines the *thickest* workpiece you can cut.

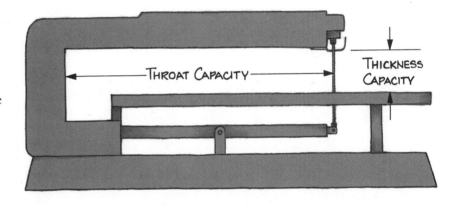

1-9 The stroke length is the vertical distance traveled by the blade. The blade must move far enough to engage several teeth in the cut, but not so far that it causes the machine to vibrate overmuch. (Each time a blade reverses direction, it produces a vibration proportional to the weight of the moving mass — the blade, blade clamps, and arms that hold them — *and* the speed at which this mass travels. Assuming that the strokes per minutes remain the same, the farther a blade moves in a single stroke, the faster it must go to cover the distance. Consequently, long strokes generate a stronger vibration.)

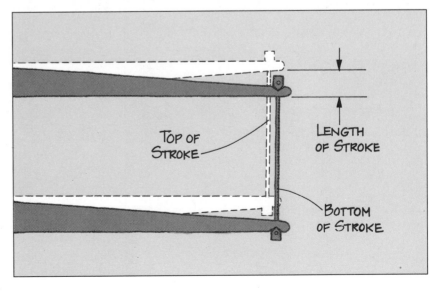

CHOOSING A SCROLL SAW

WHAT TO LOOK FOR

When purchasing a scroll saw, there are many features to consider, some obvious and some not.

Blade suspension — You want to be able to change the blades quickly and easily, without having to worry about them slipping. Quick-release blade clamps, long table slots, and a forward-mounted tension adjustment make it much easier to change the blade and thread it through the stock when making interior cuts. (*SEE FIGURES 1-10 AND 1-11.*) Removable blade clamps are also handy. They make it easier to position and tighten the blades in the clamps. Also, you can purchase extra pairs of clamps and have several blades mounted and ready to go.

Also consider how the blades are held in the clamps. There are two methods (*SEE FIGURE 1-12*):

■ *Plain-end* blades are flat at the end and are pinched between the jaws of clamps.

■ *Pin-end* blades have a tiny cross pin in each end. The pins rest in a holder or hook.

Pin-end blades are easier to mount than plain-end, and they are less likely to slip out of their holders. However, plain-end blades come in a greater variety,

and because they can be threaded through much smaller holes, they allow you to do more delicate work.

Cutting motion — On parallel-arm, double-parallel link, and C-frame scroll saws, the blades travel forward and backward slightly as they move up and down, as shown in *FIGURES 1-2 AND 1-13.* It's very important that the blade move *forward* on the *downstroke* and *backward* on the *upstroke*. This combination provides the most aggressive cutting action, helps clear the sawdust from the cut, and keeps the blade cooler.

Vibration — The reciprocating motion of a scroll saw causes the machine to vibrate, which interferes with its accuracy. Excessive vibration also makes long sessions at the saw unpleasant. The most common way in which manufacturers counteract vibration is to remove weight from the moving parts of the saw

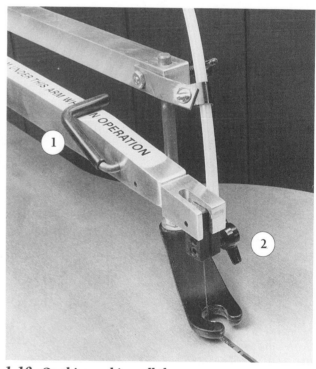

1-10 On this machine, all the controls you need to mount a blade are up front, where you can reach them easily. Furthermore, you need no wrenches or keys to operate the clamps. To apply or release the blade tension, simply throw the *tension lever* (1). To tighten or loosen the blade in its mounts, turn the *blade clamp knob* (2).

FOR BEST RESULTS

Choose a saw with blade clamps that you can operate with your fingers. When making projects that require frequent blade changes or multiple interior cuts, it's annoying to constantly have to reach for a wrench or a hex key to loosen and tighten the blade clamps. Additionally, look for flat, star, or T-shaped blade clamp knobs — these are much easier to operate. Because the knobs are small, it's difficult to get a good grip on a round one.

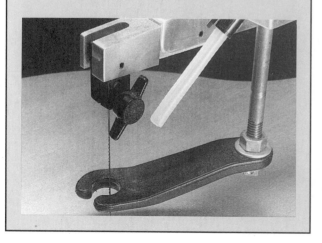

and add it to the stationary ones. Lightweight arms and blade clamps minimize vibration; heavily constructed frames and stands dampen it. Another way to prevent vibration is to move the center of gravity of the stationary mass forward, as close as possible to the center of gravity of the moving mass. This is why the motors on most well-designed scroll saws are positioned toward the front, under the table.

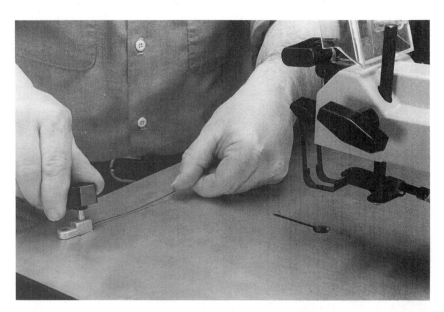

1-11 Removable blade clamps make it easier to mount blades. It's difficult to reach under a worktable, position a blade in the lower blade clamp, then hold it steady while you tighten the clamp. When you can remove the blade clamps, you can see what you're doing. Furthermore, it's easier to apply the pressure needed to keep the blade from slipping with the clamps out in the open. On some machines, only the *lower* blade clamp is removable. This isn't as convenient as being able to remove both clamps, but it's much better than not being able to remove them at all. At least you don't have to stoop down and fumble around under a worktable.

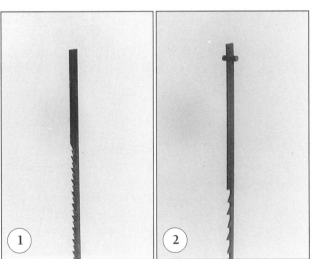

1-12 A plain-end blade (1) is secured in a blade clamp, while a *pin-end blade* (2) rests in a hook or a holder. The cross pins in pin-end blades make them easier to mount and prevent them from slipping. However, there is a greater variety of plain-end blades and they are more versatile. Consequently, the better scroll saws mount plain-end blades, while pin-end blades are reserved for hobbyists' tools. A few saws mount both types.

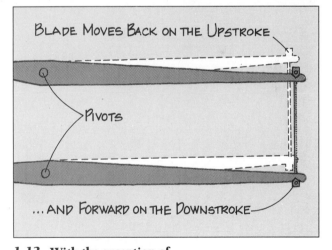

1-13 With the exception of rigid-arm (jigsaw) machines, the blades of scroll saws move backward and forward slightly in the course of a stroke. If the machine is properly designed, the blade should move *forward* on the *downstroke* as it cuts the stock, and *backward* on the *upstroke* to allow the sawdust to clear. Surprisingly, there are a few saws that work in just the opposite fashion. Although these machines cut wood, they're slower and less precise than they could be.

Recently, toolmakers have begun to attack the vibration problem from another angle, balancing the inertial forces that cause it. The double-parallel link mechanism is an example of this approach. So is the *counterbalance,* a device used on some parallel-arm, C-frame, and jigsaw machines. The eccentric that drives the pitman arm has an off-center weight (the counterbalance) opposite the attachment point for the pitman. As the drive train pushes the moving parts up, an equal amount of weight travels down. *(SEE FIGURE 1-14.)*

Among the other features that help reduce vibration are tight bearings with little play, a direct-drive motor with no pulleys or V-belt, and a stable base or a stand (with either levelers or just three feet so the saw rests squarely on the floor or workbench).

Note: The less a machine vibrates, the more quietly it runs. Reduced noise levels are a real blessing if you're going to work with a scroll saw for long periods of time.

TRY THIS TRICK

Before you buy a stationary saw, try it without the machine attached to its stand. Sometimes a heavy stand disguises a vibration-prone saw.

Tight construction — Push the blade guides right and left to check the arms for side-to-side play. There should be almost none. Also turn on the saw and watch for misaligned blade guides and blade wobble. From the front, the moving blade should appear as a straight black line, not a blur. *(SEE FIGURE 1-15.)* Excessive play, misalignment, and wobble all interfere with accuracy and cause wear and tear on the blades.

Look for machines with pivot pins fixed in the arms and pivot bushings in the frame. This arrangement provides better support than an arrangement with a single bushing in each arm. Don't be taken in by advertisements touting ball bearings. Ball bearings are designed for rotation, not reciprocation. Bushings are actually better in this application.

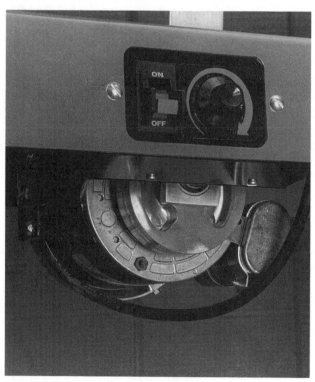

1-14 The eccentric on this scroll saw has been machined so most of its weight is on the opposite side of the motor shaft from the pitman arm. When the pitman is traveling up, most of the eccentric is traveling down. The inertial forces of the two moving parts counterbalance one another and help to reduce vibration.

1-15 A saw's moving blade should appear as a vertical black line when viewed from the front. Side-to-side play in the arm bushings will cause the blade to wobble, making it appear blurred. The blade will also appear blurred if the blade clamps are misaligned — that is, if the bottom clamp is to the right or left of the top one. **Note:** You can usually realign the blade guides to cure *small* problems with misalignment.

Variable speed — It's very handy to be able to adjust the speed from high (1,200–1,800 spm) to low (400–800 spm) to compensate for the type of blade, hardness of the material, and delicacy of the work. However, it's not necessary for the saw to have a full range of speeds between 400 and 1,800 spm. Two speeds (high and low) are probably all you need. Electronically operated speed controls are easier to use than step pulleys. *(See Figure 1-16.)* The motor switch and speed control should be up front, within easy reach.

For Your Information

The faster a saw runs (the more strokes per minute), the faster it will cut. If time is important, look for a fast-running saw.

Work support — The worktable must be large enough to properly support the work. Usually, the larger, the better — even if you don't need the size, extra mass helps dampen vibrations. A tilting table is handy, provided it's relatively easy to change angles and the table feels solid when locked in position. Pivoting tables usually work smoother than those with curved trunnions that slide in a trough, but there are a few exceptions.

Blower — Many scroll saws incorporate blowers to direct a steady stream of air at the point where the blade meets the work. This helps clear sawdust from the layout lines. *(See Figure 1-17.)* For some reason, most manufacturers mount the tube so it points forward and blows sawdust all over the front of your shirt. And very few machines have an adjustable tube so you can point the air stream where you need it.

Hold-down — The hold-down should be adjustable, and you should be able to swing it out of the way when you don't need it or when you change blades. It should also have some spring tension. Rigid hold-downs are useless when the workpiece isn't perfectly uniform in thickness. *(See Figure 1-18.)*

Safety — For some reason, several scroll saw manufacturers have yet to add guards and covers to their saws. This is unfortunate, since there are dangerous

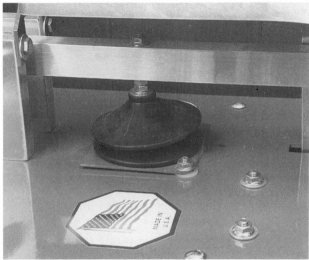

1-17 The lower arm on this scroll saw is hooked to a bellows. When the saw is turned on, the arm pumps the bellows up and down, producing a steady stream of air. The air is directed through a tube to blow away the sawdust that would otherwise obscure the pattern lines. Without a blower, you must constantly brush or blow away the dust as you work.

1-16 A variable speed control, shown on the left, is handy; but all you really need are two speeds, high (1,200–1,800 spm) and low (400–800 spm). Beware of rocker switches on two-speed saws with "Off" in the middle — these make it difficult to stop the machine in an emergency. The arrangement shown on the right, with two separate switches — one to change speeds and the other to turn the motor on and off — is much safer.

1-18 A good hold-down works
like a leaf spring, as shown on the
left. It should be adjustable, allowing
you to apply enough tension to hold
the stock on the worktable, no matter
what you're cutting. The hold-down
on the right is not adjustable, and
the tension is too light for all but the
thinnest stock. When cutting thick
plywood, as shown, it's all but useless.

pinch points on some machines. You could easily
break a finger if your hand were to slip between the
frame and the upper arm while the saw is running.
There are, however, many machines that are well
guarded. (*SEE FIGURE 1-19.*)

It's also important that the saw be designed to
protect you in case a blade breaks. On most parallel-
arm saws, a spring lifts the upper arm when the blade
snaps, preventing it from stabbing the work — or you
— before you can turn the machine off. On a jigsaw,
the spring in the rigid arm lifts the blade when it
breaks. Unfortunately, C-frame and double-parallel
link designs do not offer this protection.

Power — Surprisingly, the horsepower of the motor
that powers the scroll saw needn't be a major concern.
If you attempt to cut too fast, most likely the blade
will break before the motor bogs down. Some of the
best scroll saws only offer 1/8 horsepower.

Note: There is also one people-powered scroll
saw still available. The Tool Company of Raymond,
Missouri, makes an updated version of the old
Velocipede shown on page 2.

Finally, consider all these features in light of the
type and the *amount* of work you will be doing. If
you, like most woodworkers, have only an occasional
use for a scroll saw, you probably don't need a stationary machine that runs as smooth as glass. A benchtop
tool that vibrates slightly will save you money and
shop space. But if you plan to use a scroll saw often,
or make projects that require long periods of time at
the saw, a little vibration will quickly prove wearing.
Choose a smooth-running saw with as many user-
friendly features as you can find.

One last bit of advice: Try out as many scroll saws
as you can before you buy. Don't presume that because

you pay big bucks, you're getting a top-notch saw.
Curiously, there isn't a strong correlation between
the price of a saw and how well it performs. The
quality seems to depend more on when the machine
was designed — newer models are often better
engineered. Also consider *building* your own scroll
saw, especially if you have only an occasional use for
one. It's not difficult to make a saw that compares
favorably with many of the machines now on the
market — refer to the "Shop-Made Scroll Saw" on
page 74 for plans and instructions.

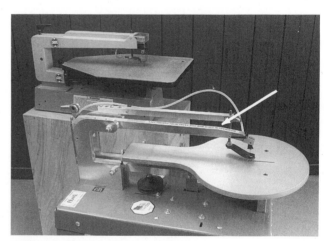

1-19 On the scroll saw in front,
you could easily pinch your fingers
between the arm and the frame if
you're not careful. Furthermore, the
blade isn't guarded. On the scroll
saw in back, the frame covers the
moving arm, eliminating any pinch
points, and the hold-down incor-
porates a blade guard.

2

SCROLL SAW BLADES AND ACCESSORIES

To use your scroll saw effectively, you must be able to match the blade to the job. There are dozens of blades to choose from, differing in size, number of teeth, and several other characteristics. Each blade is designed for a *range* of applications — it will perform several tasks, sawing different materials. For any given job, there are often three or four blades that will work well. Choosing the single best blade depends on your scroll saw, your experience, and your preferences.

There are also several accessories that can make your scroll saw more effective. You can purchase add-ons to make blade changes easier, help clear away sawdust, drill holes for interior cuts, even turn the saw off and on without using your hands. Depending on the type of work you do, these accessories can be either a boon or a waste of money.

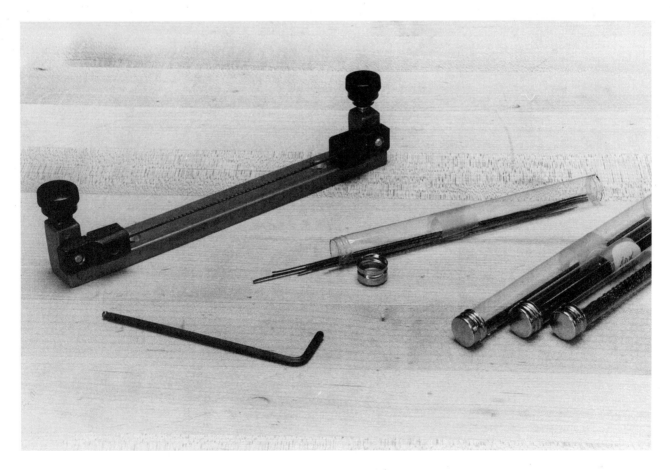

SCROLL SAW BLADES

As mentioned in Chapter 1, scroll saw blades are either *plain-end* (secured in clamps) or *pin-end* (resting in hooks or holders). Of the two, there is a much wider variety of plain-end blades. (*SEE FIGURES 2-1 AND 2-2.*)

PLAIN-END BLADES

Plain-end blades are available in different sizes, lengths, tooth styles, tooth spacings, and hardnesses.

Sizes — The size of a blade refers to its width and thickness. For the most part, blade sizes are standardized and classified according to a *Universal Numbering System* that runs from 8/0 to 12. (The larger the number, the wider and thicker the blade. For example, an 8/0 blade is .012 inch wide and .006 inch thick, while a 12 blade is .062 inch wide and .024 inch thick.) The smallest blades, 8/0 to 3/0, are intended for handsaws only. Blades between 2/0 and 12 are referred to as fret blades and are designed for use in constant-tension scroll saws. Larger blades, which are not covered by the Universal Numbering System, are called scroll blades but are intended for use on rigid-arm jigsaws — the thicker, wider blades withstand the fluctuating tension better than fret blades. Scroll blades are available in sizes up to .250 inch wide and .028 inch thick.

Note: You can use some of the smaller scroll blades in scroll saws for coarse cuts.

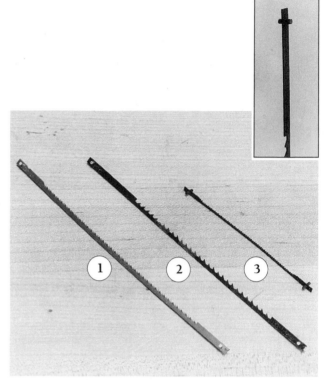

2-2 There are three types of pin-end blades: *scroll blades* (1) for coarse cutting, *fret blades* (2) for smoother and more intricate cuts, and short *hobby blades* (3) for light-duty scroll saws.

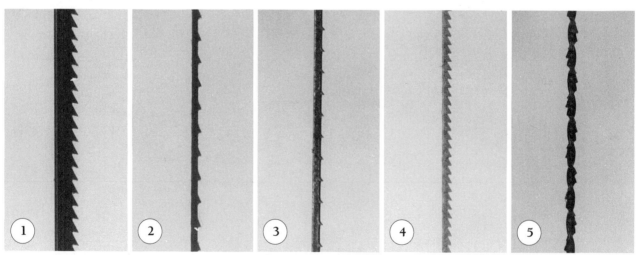

2-1 There are five types of plain-end blades available: *scroll blades* (1) for cutting wood and metals on jigsaws, *fret blades* (2) for cutting wood and other soft materials on constant-tension scroll saws, *precision-ground blades* (3) for extremely clean cuts and better control on scroll saws, *metal-cutting blades* (4) for cutting metals on scroll saws, and standard-tooth *spiral blades* (5) for omnidirectional cutting of wood and metals on scroll saws. Each blade type comes in a variety of sizes with different tooth spacing. Fret blades are available with different tooth styles as well.

Lengths — Most plain-end blades are 5 inches long and will fit almost all scroll saws and jigsaws. A few coarse-cutting scroll blades are 6 inches long. These are specially made for cutting stock over 2 inches thick and are used mostly in heavy-duty industrial jigsaws with strokes over 1¼ inches long.

Tooth style — There are three different tooth styles — *standard, skip-tooth,* and *double-skip tooth. (See* FIGURE 2-3.)

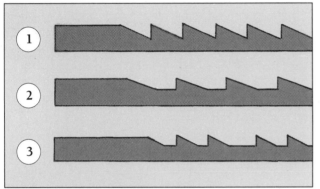

2-3 There are three different tooth styles for saw blades. *Standard teeth* (1) are spaced close together and are used mostly for large scroll blades and metal-cutting blades. *Skip teeth* (2) are used for fine fret blades. They make fast cuts in wood and other soft materials. So do *double-skip teeth* (3), but they cut slower and leave a slightly smoother surface than ordinary skip teeth.

■ Standard teeth are arranged close together and are used mostly on large scroll (jigsaw) blades and finer metal-cutting blades. On a large blade with standard teeth, the *gullets* (the spaces between the teeth) are wide enough to clear the sawdust as the teeth cut the wood. On a smaller metal-cutting blade, the gullets are smaller, but so are the metal shavings, and the blade doesn't clog. However, if you were to use a small blade with standard teeth to cut wood, the gullets would quickly pack with sawdust. This, in turn, would cause the blade to overheat and break.

■ Skip teeth are spaced farther apart and have larger gullets between them to help clear the waste from the cut. Most fret blades have skip teeth — this helps them run cooler and cut faster.

■ Double-skip teeth have both large and small gullets, alternating along the length of the blade. They cut a little slower than ordinary skip teeth, but they clear the waste from a cut reasonably well, stay fairly cool, and leave a slightly smoother cut. Like skip teeth, they are intended for cutting wood and are used mostly on fret blades.

Another variation is the *reverse skip-tooth blade. (See* FIGURE 2-4.) It has ordinary skip teeth, but the last few teeth near the bottom end of the blade are reversed. This arrangement prevents splintering and tear-out on the bottom of the cut. The blade is especially useful for cutting plywood and softwoods. **Note:** In catalogs and charts, reverse skip-tooth blades are denoted with an "R" following the universal number.

2-4 Skip-tooth fret blades are available with *reverse teeth*. The last few teeth at the bottom of the blade point up. When the blade is mounted on a scroll saw, two or three of these teeth come up above the table at the top of each stroke. This helps to control *feathering* — the tiny splinters and tear-outs that occur on the bottom surface of the workpiece. The plywood on the bottom was cut with an ordinary skip-tooth blade, while the one on the top was cut with a reverse skip-tooth blade. As you can see, the reverse teeth do not completely eliminate the feathers, but they do reduce them substantially.

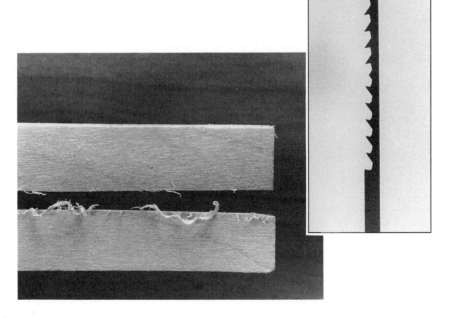

Tooth spacing — The number of *teeth per inch* (tpi) on a blade depends on its size and tooth style. *(SEE FIGURE 2-5.)* Larger blades have bigger teeth and fewer of them. For example, a number 5 blade has 36 standard tpi, while a number 12 has just 20. Double-skip tooth blades have fewer teeth than standard ones, and skip-tooth blades have the fewest of all. A number 5 double-skip tooth blade has 16 tpi, and a number 5 skip-tooth has 12½, compared to 36 tpi on a standard blade.

Hardness — All scroll saw blades are made from tool steel. Metal-cutting blades are also hardened and tempered to help them stay sharp when cutting hard materials. But scroll blades and fret blades that are intended to cut soft materials (such as wood, plastic, and bone) aren't usually treated.

There is an important difference between *metal-cutting* and *metal-piercing* blades. Metal-piercing blades are much smaller — as tiny as 8/0 or .012 inch wide and .006 inch thick. They are intended to be used only in hand tools such as jeweller's saws and fret saws. Blades this small are too delicate and brittle to be used safely in a scroll saw or jigsaw. Their minuscule gullets quickly become packed with waste, and the blade soon snaps. Metal-cutting blades aren't as fine as metal-piercing ones — they start with universal number 1, or .024 inch wide by .012 inch thick.

They are also tempered differently, so they aren't as brittle. This and their larger size help them stand up to the abuse of a power saw.

There are also two specialty blades available with plain ends:

■ *Spiral blades* are twisted standard-tooth blades that cut in all directions — you can cut sharp corners without turning the stock. *(SEE FIGURE 2-6.)* Spiral blades are hardened and tempered and can be used to cut nonferrous metals as well as wood and other soft materials.

■ *Precision-ground blades* are skip-tooth fret blades that have been ground rather than milled or stamped. The normal process for cutting teeth leaves many small burrs, while the grinding process doesn't. *(SEE FIGURE 2-7.)* Ground teeth are much sharper and stay that way longer. They cut faster, leave a smoother surface, and give you better control.

2-6 A spiral blade *(left)* will cut in all directions. Because of this, it will turn a much sharper corner than an ordinary fret blade *(right)*. Furthermore, it will make turns without your having to turn the stock; just change the direction of the feed. Spiral blades are especially useful when you need to cut a pattern that's too large in one direction for the throat of your saw. If the short dimension will fit, a spiral blade enables you to saw the pattern without turning the workpiece. The disadvantages are that these blades are tricky to use and that they leave a much wider kerf than others.

2-5 The number of teeth per inch (tpi) indicates not only the tooth spacing, but also the *size* of the teeth. The greater the tpi, the smaller the teeth. This gives you an indication of how the blade will cut. The smaller the teeth (and the greater the tpi), the slower and smoother the blade will cut.

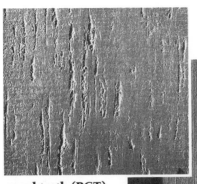

2-7 Precision-ground teeth (PGT) are cut with a process that leaves them much sharper than ordinary milled teeth. Consequently, PGT fret blades cut faster and leave a smoother surface than the ordinary variety. They also give you better control. The wood on the left was cut with a precision-ground blade. When magnified 25 times, the surface appears smoother and has fewer "whiskers" (ragged fibers) than the wood on the right, which was cut with an ordinary blade. *Micrographs courtesy of George F. Vander Voort, Carpenter Technology, Reading, Pa.*

Try This Trick

If you need a large selection of blades, keep them organized in a holder made from 4-inch lengths of ½-inch PVC pipe. Cut as many pieces of pipe as you need, and drill holes in a wooden base to hold them upright. Label each pipe so you know what blade is stored in it. Without some sort of system for organization, blades can become hopelessly mixed.

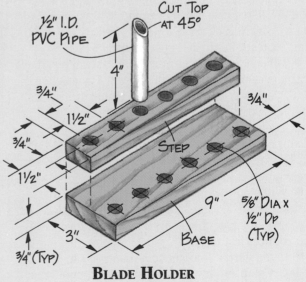

BLADE HOLDER

PIN-END BLADES

Pin-end blades are also available in two lengths —
2¾ and 5 inches long. (The shorter blades are used
in light-duty, small-capacity scroll saws, sometimes
referred to as *hobby saws.*) However, they come in
only a few sizes — the smallest are as wide as a number 12 plain-end fret blade, and the largest as wide as
a small scroll blade. (They seem to fill the gap between
the two.) And there are just two tooth styles in pin-end
blades: standard and skip-tooth.

Although there are fewer sizes and styles to choose
from, pin-end blades do offer several advantages. They
are extremely easy to mount; all you have to do is
position the pins in the holders and apply tension.
(With a plain-end blade, you have to hold each end in
position while you tighten the clamps, then apply tension.) And once mounted, pin-end blades won't slip.
This makes them useful for coarse-cutting thick stock.

CHOOSING BLADES

How do you know which blade is best for a particular
job? There are several rules of thumb for choosing
blades.

■ Always use the largest blade (the highest universal number) that will make the cut. A blade that's too
small will take longer and dull sooner.

■ Generally, the thicker the workpiece you want to
cut, the larger the blade should be. Larger blades are
stiffer and able to withstand more pressure. Smaller
blades not only flex more but also tend to overheat
when cutting thick stock.

■ The blade mustn't be too large, however. There
should be at least *three teeth in contact with the wood* as
you saw. (*See Figure 2-8.*) For example, if you want to
cut a ¼-inch-thick piece of wood, use a blade with at
least 12 teeth per inch — one-fourth of 12 is 3.

■ When cutting an intricate shape, always start
with the coarsest cuts and the biggest blades, then
work your way down to fine cuts with small blades.
In other words, rough out the shape first, then fill in
the details. Even though you may have to change
blades two or three times as you saw, the work will
progress much faster than if you were trying to cut
the whole shape with a tiny blade.

■ When cutting plywood, veneer, or stock that
easily splinters or tears out on the bottom surface, use
a reverse-tooth fret blade. As mentioned previously,
this reduces feathering.

■ If you need a smoother cut than you can get from
ordinary skip-tooth blades, try ones with double-skip
teeth.

■ For ultrasmooth cuts or better control, use
precision-ground blades. PGT blades are much more
expensive than other blades, but the cut surface looks
as if it has been polished. And because the teeth are
so sharp, it's easier to follow the pattern lines.

■ You don't need a huge selection of blades.
Experienced craftsmen often make do with just five
or six types, and find themselves using just a couple
of these for 90 percent of their work.

What blades are used most often? Retailers report
that 5, 7, and 9 are the most popular sizes. If you're
just starting out, purchase number 5R and 12 skip-
tooth fret blades for general cutting, number 2 fret
blades for intricate work in thin materials, a precision-
ground blade with 10 tpi for smooth cuts, and a number 7 metal-cutting blade for occasional work with
soft metals. Get a little experience with these blades,
then expand your selection once you have a good
idea of what works best for you.

2-8 Always select the *largest*
(widest and thickest) blade that will
do the job, while making sure there
are enough teeth. At least *two,* preferably *three,* teeth should remain in
contact with the wood as you cut. To
check that you've selected the right
blade, multiply the thickness of the
workpiece (in inches) by the tpi number. If the answer is less than 3, use a
smaller blade with more teeth per
inch. In a pinch, you can make do
with fewer teeth in the cut, but the
work may be more difficult to control.

Scroll Saw and Jigsaw Blades

		PLAIN-END BLADES			
	UNIVERSAL NUMBER	WIDTH	THICKNESS	TPI	APPLICATIONS
Skip-Tooth Fret Blades *(for scroll saws)*	2/0 0	.022″ .024″	.010″ .011″	28 25	Very intricate cuts in veneer, plastics, and other thin, soft materials 1/16″ to 1/4″ thick
	2 4	.029″ .035″	.012″ .015″	20 15	Small-radius cuts in veneer, wood, plastic, and soft materials 3/32″ to 1/2″ thick
	5 6	.038″ .041″	.016″ .016″	12.5 12.5	Medium-radius cuts in wood, plastic, and soft materials 1/8″ to 1″ thick
	7 9 11 12	.045″ .053″ .059″ .062″	.017″ .018″ .019″ .024″	11.5 11.5 9.5 9.5	General cutting in wood, plastic, and soft materials 3/16″ to 2″ thick
	– – –	.080″ .070″ .070″	.010″ .010″ .014″	14 18.5 18.5	Straight or gently curved cuts requiring extremely thin kerfs in soft materials 3/32″ to 1/2″ thick
	– –	.090″ .110″	.022″ .022″	7 7	Coarse cuts in wood and plastic 1/2″ to 2″ thick
Precision Ground Skip-Tooth Fret Blades *(for scroll saws)*	– – –	.040″ .046″ .048″	.018″ .018″ .018″	12 10 8	Smooth cuts and precise control in soft materials 1/4″ to 2″ thick
Double-Skip Tooth Fret Blades *(for scroll saws)*	1	.026″	.013″	30	Smooth, intricate cuts in soft materials 1/16″ to 1/4″ thick
	3	.032″	.014″	23	Smooth, small-radius cuts in soft materials 3/32″ to 1/2″ thick
	5	.038″	.016″	16	Smooth, medium-radius cuts in soft materials 1/8″ to 1″ thick
	7 9 12	.044″ .053″ .061″	.018″ .018″ .022″	13 11 10	Smooth, general cuts in soft materials 3/16″ to 2″ thick

(continued) ▷

SCROLL SAW AND JIGSAW BLADES — CONTINUED

PLAIN-END BLADES					
	UNIVERSAL NUMBER	WIDTH	THICKNESS	TPI	APPLICATIONS
Reverse Skip-Tooth Fret Blades *(for scroll saws)*	5R	.038″	.016″	12.5	Reduction of splintering and feathered edges when cutting wood and plywood
	7R	.047″	.017″	11.5	
	12R	.062″	.024″	9.5	
	–	.100″	.022″	9	
Standard-Tooth Metal-Cutting Blades *(for scroll saws)*	1	.024″	.012″	48	Cutting metals from .060″ thick and other hard materials from 1/16″ thick
	5	.033″	.016″	36	
	7	.041″	.019″	30	
	9	.049″	.022″	25	
	12	.070″	.023″	20	
Standard-Tooth Scroll Blades *(for jigsaws)*	–	.110″	.022″	20	Cutting wood
	–	.250″	.028″	20	Cutting metals and other hard materials
	–	.110″	.022″	15	Cutting wood, wood products, and other soft materials
	–	.110″	.022″	10	Cutting wood and plastic
	–	.187″	.025″	10	
	–	.250″	.028″	7	

	UNIVERSAL NUMBER	KERF WIDTH	TPI	APPLICATIONS
Standard-Tooth Spiral Blades *(for scroll saws)*	2/0	.030″	51	Omnidirectional cuts in wood, wood products, plastic, and other soft materials 1/16″ to 1″ thick; can also be used to cut nonferrous metals
	0	.032″	46	
	1	.034″	46	
	2	.035″	41	
	3	.037″	41	
	4	.041″	36	
	5	.047″	36	
	6	.051″	30	

PIN-END BLADES

	UNIVERSAL NUMBER	WIDTH	THICKNESS	TPI	APPLICATIONS
Skip-Tooth Fret Blades *(for scroll saws)*	–	.070″	.010″	18.5	Cutting wood and plastic ³/₃₂″ to ¹/₂″ thick
	–	.070″	.014″	18.5	
	–	.100″	.018″	9	Cutting wood and wood products
Standard-Tooth Scroll Blades *(for jigsaws)*	–	.070″	.010″	25	Cutting wood and plastic ³/₃₂″ to ¹/₂″ thick
	–	.110″	.018″	20	Cutting wood
	–	.110″	.018″	15	Cutting wood, wood products, and other soft materials
	–	.110″	.018″	10	Cutting wood and plastic
Skip-Tooth Hobby Blades *(2³/₄″ long — for hobby saws)*	–	.068″	.014″	18.5	Cutting wood and plastic
	–	.150″	.015″	15	
Standard-Tooth Hobby Blades *(2³/₄″ long — for hobby saws)*	–	.068″	.010″	25	Cutting wood, plastic, and nonferrous metals

SCROLL SAW ACCESSORIES

Scroll saws and blades have changed tremendously in the last twenty years, becoming much more capable and easier to use. As they have evolved, manufacturers have also created accessories that will increase the capability of a saw or make it more user-friendly. Some of these are retrofits for older saws to bring them up-to-date. Others are add-ons that may improve any saw, old or new. And a few of them are useless, no matter what kind of saw you use them with.

Among the most useful accessories are *quick-release blade clamps*. In the past, most scroll saws required a hex key or special wrench to operate the blade clamps. Today, more and more toolmakers are offering models with blade clamps that you can release or tighten with your fingers. If your saw isn't fitted with these, you may be able to update it — quick-release blade clamps are available for Excalibur, Delta, Hegner, RBI, and most of the imported Taiwanese-made saws.

Many of the knobs on quick-release blade clamps are round and are hard to hold on to. Engineers do this for a reason — a round knob prevents you from applying too much pressure and splitting the clamp. However, if you change blades often, the round knobs begin to wear on your fingertips. Look for quick-release blade clamps with flat, T-shaped, or star knobs. These provide a more comfortable grasp. (*SEE FIGURES 2-9 AND 2-10.*)

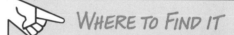

WHERE TO FIND IT

You can purchase quick-release blade clamps for most popular brands of scroll saws from:

Seyco
1414 Cranford Drive
Box 472749
Garland, TX 75047

Advanced Machinery Imports Ltd.
P.O. Box 312
New Castle, DE 19720

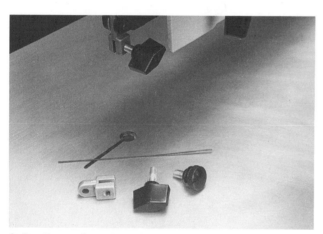

2-9 Flat, T-shaped, and star knobs are easier to grip and more comfortable to use than round ones. For this reason, you may want to replace the round knobs in your blade clamps, as was done here. Look for knobs with threaded studs — specialty knobs of many different shapes are available from hardware stores and mail-order woodworking suppliers. If you can't find knobs that fit your saw, make them. The flat knobs shown originally had no studs, just threaded inserts and these were the wrong size. We cut the threaded portions from bolts to make studs of the proper size, drilled and tapped the inserts, and secured the new studs in the knobs with epoxy.

2-10 If you can't replace your round knobs, drill several $^{3}/_{16}$-inch-diameter holes in the circumferences, as shown. The holes enable you to insert a $^{5}/_{32}$-inch allen wrench in the knob whenever you need a bit more leverage to tighten or loosen the clamp. Whether you use shaped knobs or round knobs with holes in them, be careful not to apply too much pressure when you tighten them — you don't want to split the clamps.

Blade-changing fixtures enable you to mount blades in removable blade clamps without first having to secure the clamps on the saw. *(SEE FIGURE 2-11.)* If you have more than one pair of blade clamps, you can keep extra blades mounted and ready to use. A few saws come with these fixtures, but they're usually offered by the manufacturer as an extra.

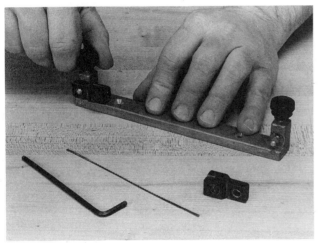

2-11 If you have removable blade clamps and need to change blades often, a blade-changing fixture and a few extra pairs of clamps can be handy. The fixture enables you to mount a blade in the clamps and get it ready to cut without having to secure the clamps in the saw.

Most new saw models include blowers to clear the sawdust away from the pattern line as you cut. If your saw is not fitted with a blower, you can purchase a *blower kit* that will fit most scroll saws from some mail-order woodworking suppliers.

TRY THIS TRICK

Pick up an *aquarium pump* at any pet store and use it as a blower for your scroll saw. Make a blower nozzle from a piece of soft copper tubing. Crimp or flatten the end slightly, reducing the area of the tube opening to increase the velocity of the air as it exits the nozzle.

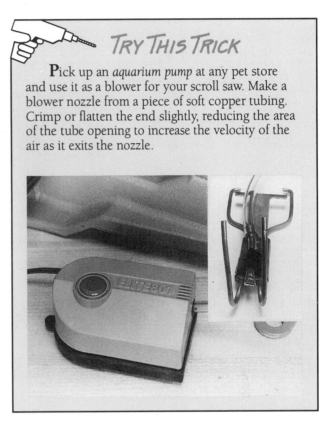

TRY THIS TRICK

Make your own blade-changing fixture from a few scraps of hardwood. Cutouts in the plate hold the clamps while you tighten the locking screws.

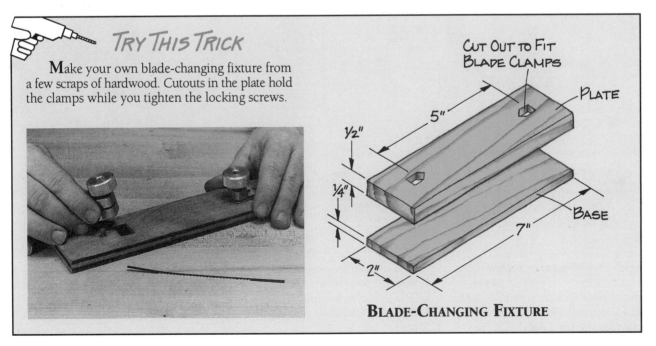

BLADE-CHANGING FIXTURE

A *magnifier lamp* not only throws light directly on your work, it magnifies the pattern lines slightly. (*SEE FIGURE 2-12.*) The lamp makes it much easier to see what you're sawing and is especially useful for intricate fretwork and marquetry. You can also use a *loupe* or a *headband magnifier* to help you see the pattern.

A few scroll saws offer a *flexible shaft tool* as an accessory. One end of the shaft hooks to the scroll saw motor, and the other has a chuck that will hold small sanding drums, rasps, and drills. It's of limited use in scroll saw work, unless you use it to drill holes to thread blades through the workpiece. You can also purchase a *drilling attachment* — a miniature drill press that fastens to the scroll saw frame — that will perform the same function. (*SEE FIGURE 2-13.*) However, neither of these is as versatile (or as inexpensive) as a cordless drill. If you need to shoot holes as you work, keep a drill next to your scroll saw.

2-12 Because scroll saw work is often very intricate, it helps to have a light that you can shine right on the worktable. A magnifier lamp is doubly useful. It not only illuminates the pattern lines, it also magnifies them so you can see them more easily.

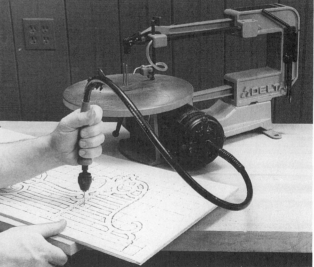

2-13 A drilling attachment (left) fastens directly to your scroll saw and enables you to shoot holes while you work. A flexible shaft tool (right) provides the same capability. However, neither of these attachments is as versatile as a cordless drill, which will do the same job plus a good deal more. *Photo (left) courtesy of Seyco.*

A *foot switch* frees up both of your hands and makes it easier to operate a scroll saw. (SEE FIGURE 2-14.) It's especially useful if you are doing a fretwork project that requires you to turn the saw on and off continually.

Finally, there is one accessory that simply does not do what it is supposed to — *anti-vibration pads* are not effective. Despite the claims of advertisers, rubber or felt pads don't reduce the vibration of the machine, they only *isolate* it. The pads work much the same as the rubber engine mounts in your car — the mounts isolate the engine vibration from the chassis, without reducing it. (SEE FIGURE 2-15.) If you want to reduce the vibration of your scroll saw, attach it to a heavy stand, or mount it on the "Sand Base" shown on page 26.

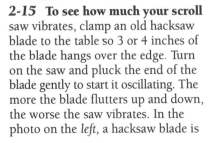

2-14 Having to constantly reach under the worktable to turn the scroll saw on and off can slow you down during a long work session. A foot switch eliminates this annoyance.

> ☞ FOR BEST RESULTS
>
> **I**f you use a benchtop scroll saw on your workbench, position it directly over a leg — this will help disperse the vibrations throughout the workbench frame. And if your scroll saw or scroll saw stand has rubber feet, remove them. These work like anti-vibration pads to isolate the vibration rather than reduce it.

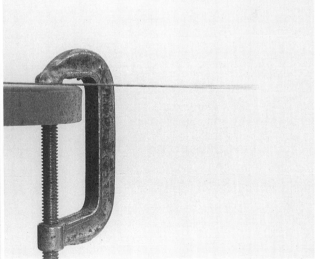

2-15 To see how much your scroll saw vibrates, clamp an old hacksaw blade to the table so 3 or 4 inches of the blade hangs over the edge. Turn on the saw and pluck the end of the blade gently to start it oscillating. The more the blade flutters up and down, the worse the saw vibrates. In the photo on the *left*, a hacksaw blade is clamped to a benchtop scroll saw mounted on an anti-vibration pad. As you can see, the saw vibrates considerably; the pad has done nothing to dampen the vibration. The photo on the *right* shows the same blade clamped to the same scroll saw, but the saw is now mounted on a sand base. There is almost no vibration.

SAND BASE

Using sand to reduce vibration is an old turner's trick. To make their lathes run as smooth as possible, savvy turners bury the feet of the lathe stand in sand, or discard the stand altogether and mount the power tool on sturdy boxes filled with sand.

This base is designed to do the same thing for a scroll saw. It's nothing more than a box filled with sand. Bolt the scroll saw on top of the box. As the saw runs and the sand compacts, the vibrations will affect the worktable less and less.

1 **Fill the box with sand to** within 1 inch of the top edge. Level the sand as much as you can, then place the lid over the studs. The lid should fit within the sides of the box and rest on the sand. Then place the scroll saw on the lid so its base fits over the studs, too. Put washers and nuts on the ends of the studs.

2 **Turn on the scroll saw and** let it run — the vibrations will begin to compact the sand. Tighten the nuts, let the saw run for a few minutes more, and tighten them again. As the sand compacts, the lid will settle down on its surface. After a bit, the nuts will be as tight as they're going to get and the vibrations should be substantially reduced. To reduce them even further, clamp or fasten the base to a bench or stand.

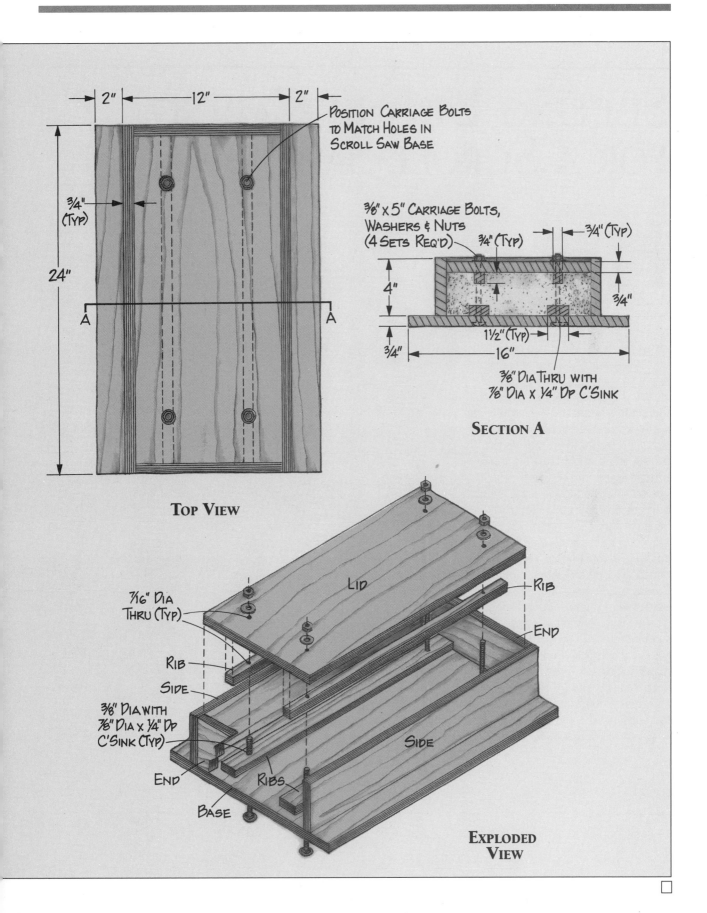

2" 12" 2"

POSITION CARRIAGE BOLTS
TO MATCH HOLES IN
SCROLL SAW BASE

¾"
(TYP)

24"

A   A

TOP VIEW

⅜" x 5" CARRIAGE BOLTS,
WASHERS & NUTS
(4 SETS REQ'D)

¾" (TYP)   ¾" (TYP)

4"

¾"

¾"   1½" (TYP)

16"

⅜" DIA THRU WITH
⅞" DIA x ¼" DP C'SINK

SECTION A

⁷⁄₁₆" DIA
THRU (TYP)

LID

RIB

RIB

END

SIDE

⅜" DIA WITH
⅞" DIA x ¼" DP
C'SINK (TYP)

SIDE

END

RIBS

BASE

**EXPLODED
VIEW**

3

SETTING UP AND CARING FOR A SCROLL SAW

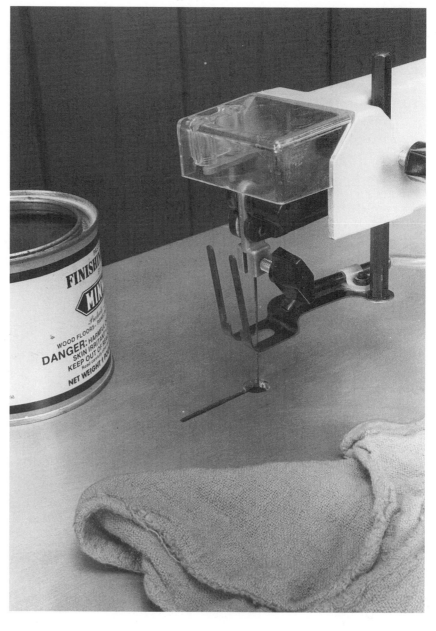

How well a scroll saw cuts depends not only on the quality of the machine and the type of blade, but also on how you set up the tool before you begin. Like any power tool, the scroll saw must be properly aligned and adjusted — you have to mount the blade straight in the clamps, apply the correct amount of tension, and tilt the worktable at the proper angle to the blade. If you're using a blade for the first time, you may need to remove the metal burrs on the teeth or round the back corners.

For a scroll saw to continue to cut well, it must be well maintained. The reciprocating motion is hard on the machine, much harder than rotary motion. And the fine dust generated by the saw can interfere with moving parts and electrical contacts. So it's vital to inspect your scroll saw frequently, keep it clean, and lubricate it now and then to maintain it in top running order.

ALIGNMENT AND ADJUSTMENT

There is surprisingly little alignment and adjustment to do on scroll saws; almost all the critical relationships between the moving parts are set permanently during manufacturing. For everyday operations, all you have to do is mount the blade, apply tension to it, and adjust the angle of the worktable to the blade.

MOUNTING A BLADE

The procedure for mounting a blade is different for every scroll saw. It depends on the design of the clamps and the type of blade used. However, a few important considerations are always the same.

As you fasten a plain-end blade in place, you must make sure that the blade is straight in the clamps, then tighten the clamp jaws sufficiently so the blade doesn't slip when you tension it. (SEE FIGURES 3-1 AND 3-2.) If you have removable blade clamps, use a blade-changing fixture to mount the blade. (SEE FIGURE 3-3.) It holds the clamps steady while you turn the wrench or the key, making it easier to apply the necessary pressure.

Make sure that the teeth *face down,* toward the worktable. If you accidentally mount the blade upside down, the workpiece will lift off the table with every upstroke. Also consider whether the teeth should face forward or to one side. Some scroll saws, particularly those that mount pin-end blades, let you orient a blade right, left, or forward. This allows you to make cuts in workpieces that might otherwise be too large for the throat capacity of your machine.

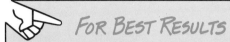

FOR BEST RESULTS

If you must apply a great deal of pressure to keep your blades from slipping, check that the clamps are clean. A little bit of sawdust can prevent the clamp jaw from getting a good grip.

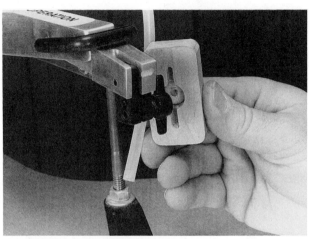

3-2 Quick-release blade clamps usually can be tightened and loosened with the fingers. But if you find the knobs are too small to grip, or if your fingers are too weak to apply sufficient pressure, make a wrench from a piece of scrap wood to fit over the knobs. **Warning:** *Don't fasten wooden wrenches to the knobs to enlarge them permanently. This adds weight to the ends of the arms and increases the vibration of the machine.*

3-1 When you mount a plain-end blade, push it all the way to the back of the clamp and make sure that it hangs *straight.* If the blade is held toward the front of the clamp or at an angle, it's much more likely to slip. And even if the blade doesn't slip, it will bow toward the front or the back, become fatigued, and break much sooner than normal.

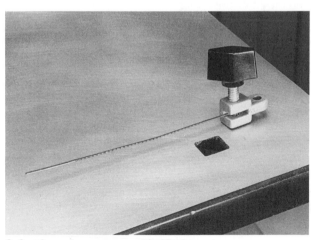

TRY THIS TRICK

If you need to turn a blade so the teeth face right or left, but the blade clamps aren't designed to do this, use a spiral blade. If you can't substitute a spiral blade, twist the blade ends with needlenose pliers so the teeth face the desired direction. This fatigues the metal and shortens the life of the blade, but the blade will probably last long enough to make several cuts.

3-3 If you have removable blade clamps, you may wish to use a blade-changing fixture to hold them while you mount the blades. On some machines, such as the Shopsmith shown, these are built into or attached to the worktable. Although it's not always necessary to use these fixtures, they make it easier to position the blades straight in the clamps and apply the required pressure.

If you use a blade with reverse teeth, position it so only two or three teeth rise above the table at the top of the upstroke. (SEE FIGURE 3-4.) If you have too many reverse teeth rising above the table, they will lift the work off the table just as if you had mounted the blade upside down.

TENSIONING THE BLADE

Once you've mounted the blade, you must apply tension to it. The tensioning adjustment device is different for every saw. On some, it's located in the back; on others it's towards the front. On some you turn a knob or screw; on others you throw a lever or a cam. The purpose is always the same — to create enough tension to hold the blade rigid as it cuts. Without sufficient tension, the slender blade would flex or bow.

How much tension should you apply? Blade manufacturers recommend 20,000 to 30,000 pounds per square inch (psi). This sounds like a lot, but consider how many blades you could fit in that square inch.

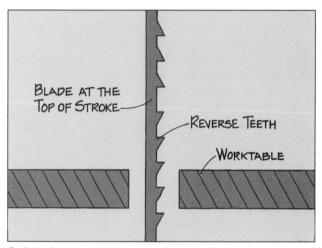

3-4 When using a reverse skip-tooth blade, position it in the clamps so only two or three teeth rise above the table at the top of the stroke. Usually, you can do this by simply sliding the blade up or down in the clamps. Sometimes, however, you must clip a little off the top or bottom end of the blade with a pair of wire cutters. One major scroll saw blade company, Olson Blades, makes its reverse-tooth blades a little long for just this reason. In extreme cases you may have to make an auxiliary table from a scrap of plywood to raise the surface of the worktable.

Because scroll saw blades are so slender and have such a minuscule cross section, this works out to 5 or 10 pounds of "pull" for most blades.

How do you know when you've applied enough tension? Unfortunately, manufacturers don't provide tension gauges on scroll saws, and there are no reasonably priced measuring devices available. Of the several techniques for estimating tension, none is very accurate. Some craftsmen pluck the blade like a guitar string as they apply tension, tuning it to a certain note (usually C above high C). Others tighten the blade until it just begins to straighten out, then turn the tension adjustment knob a certain number of turns past that. (The number of turns necessary varies from saw to saw.)

Chuck Olson, president of the Olson Blade Company, recommends this simple procedure for tensioning a blade. As you tighten the tension knob, push on the back of the blade with your index finger, applying *moderate* pressure. When you can't flex the blade horizontally any more than 1/8 inch, it's properly tensioned. (*See Figure 3-5.*)

None of these techniques tells you how much tension you're applying, but you needn't worry about it overmuch. If the blade bows or cups, or if it wanders in the cut, you know the tension is too loose. (*See Figure* 3-6.) If blades break frequently, you could be applying too much tension. As long as the blade cuts well and lasts a reasonably long time, it's properly tensioned.

ALIGNING THE BLADE CLAMPS

The manufacturer should have aligned the upper blade clamp directly over the lower one, so that the blade is held perfectly vertical. Otherwise, the blade will travel up and down at a slight skew, cutting a wider kerf than it should. (*See Figure 3-7.*)

Check the alignment when you first set up your scroll saw, and then once a year or whenever you suspect problems. To do this, place a small allen wrench or a dowel on the worktable with one end against the flat side of the blade. (The blade must be mounted and tensioned.) Rotate the eccentric by hand, slowly moving the arms through a single stroke. The blade should remain in contact with the wrench or dowel throughout the stroke. If the blade moves toward or away from it, you may need to realign the clamps. (*See Figure 3-8.*)

Before you do, however, check that the blade isn't bent and that it's mounted properly in the clamps. Also see that the clamps are clean. Sometimes a few tiny pieces of dirt or sawdust will cause the clamp to push

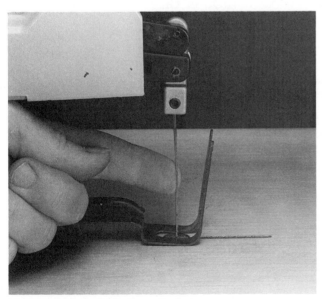

3-5 To tension a blade, tighten the tension adjustment while applying *moderate* pressure against the back of the blade with your index finger. (Don't push so hard that it hurts.) When you can't flex the blade any more than 1/8 inch, it's tight enough.

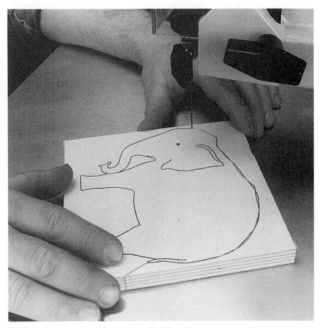

3-6 The best indicator of a loose blade is the way it cuts. If the blade wanders back and forth so that you can't follow the pattern line, add a little more tension to it.

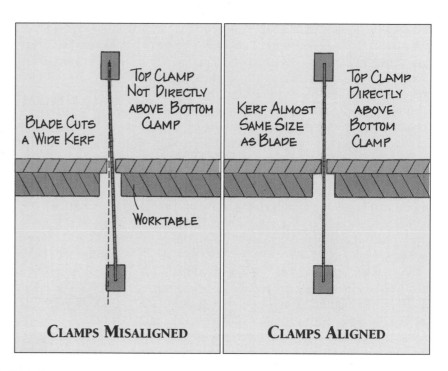

3-7 The upper blade clamp must be directly over the lower one to hold the blade vertical. If the blade is held at a slight skew, as shown on the left, the kerf it cuts will be much wider than necessary. This slows down the cutting process and puts more wear and tear on the blade, since the blade must remove more stock than it would if the clamps were properly aligned. When the blade is held precisely vertical, as shown on the right, the saw kerf is not much wider than the blade itself.

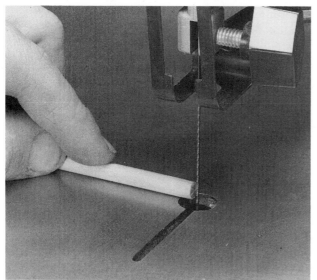

3-8 To check the blade clamp alignment, first unplug the scroll saw. Mount a large (number 12) *straight* blade and tension it. Place the end of a small allen wrench or a dowel against the flat side of the blade, as shown, to serve as an indicator. Turn the eccentric by hand through one full stroke. If the clamps are misaligned and the blade is skewed, the blade will move away from the indicator through part of the stroke, then move toward it during the remainder.

the blade to one side or the other. (*SEE FIGURE 3-9.*) If the blade is properly mounted in clean clamps, the clamps do need to be aligned.

Some scroll saws let you slide the blade guides left or right to realign them. On others, there is a small set screw on one side of each clamp that allows you to move the fixed clamp jaw about $1/16$ inch right or left. (*SEE FIGURE 3-10.*) This is a tiny amount, but it's usually all that's needed. Adjust the top or bottom set screw, or both, until the clamps hold the blade as close to vertical as you can get it. If you can't completely correct the misalignment, don't worry. You can usually live with the blade clamps *slightly* misaligned (less than $1/32$ inch) — the machine will continue to cut fairly well. **Note:** *Don't* back out the set screw so far that the fixed jaw lies below the surface of the clamp housing — it *must* protrude slightly.

A BIT OF ADVICE

Don't try to bend the arms sideways to align blade clamps that are poorly aligned. If you can't bring the clamps into close alignment by adjusting the positions of the jaws, it may be because the bushings or pivots are worn unevenly. Consult your owner's manual for what to do next — your machine may need to be serviced.

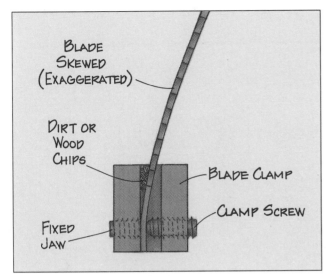

3-9   Before you adjust the blade
clamps, check that they are free of
dirt, sawdust, or other foreign matter.
Just a little bit of sawdust on the
clamp jaws could skew the blade and
make it appear that the clamps were
misaligned.

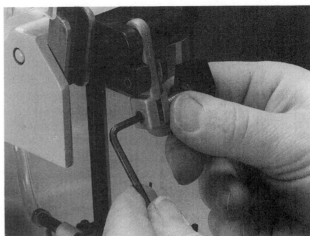

3-10   To align some blade clamps,
all you have to do is slide them right
or left. On others you must change
the positions of the fixed jaws. Look
for a set screw on the side of the
clamp, opposite the knob or the
device you use to tighten it. To move
the fixed jaw right or left, turn the
set screw.

ADJUSTING THE TABLE ANGLE

Once the blade is mounted, tensioned, and running
true, you must adjust the worktable to the proper
angle. Most saws have a scale on the table trunnion
to help set the angle, but it's always a good idea to
double-check. When you want to set the worktable at
90 degrees to the blade, use a small square to check
the alignment. (SEE FIGURE 3-11.) To set the worktable at
some other angle, use a small triangle or a protractor.
(SEE FIGURE 3-12.)

Also check the angle of the blade to the table from
front to back — it should be perfectly square, no matter how the table is tilted. (SEE FIGURE 3-13.) If it isn't,
the blade isn't properly mounted. **Note:** If you have
a C-frame saw, don't bother to check this angle — it
changes throughout the stroke. However, you may
wish to use a small square or straightedge to check
that the back of the blade is straight, not bowed or
bent.

TRY THIS TRICK

You can also use a piece of scrap wood to check
that the table is square to the blade. Make a shallow
cut in one surface, then turn the scrap around (but
don't turn it upside down) and try to slip the back of
the blade into the cut. If the blade slips into the cut
without your having to raise one side of the scrap off
the table, the table is square to the blade.

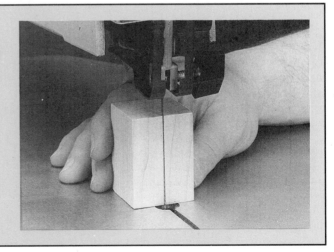

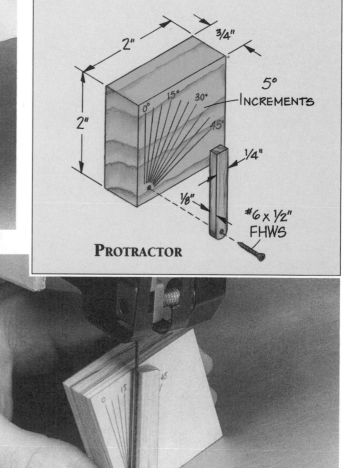

PROTRACTOR

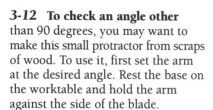

3-11 The vast majority of scroll saw cuts are made with the work-table square to the blade. To check this angle, rest a small square on the table and hold one arm against the flat side of the blade. If you can see any daylight between the blade and the square, adjust the table angle. **Note:** If you do a lot of scroll work, you may want to buy a 2-inch engineer's square for this task.

3-12 To check an angle other than 90 degrees, you may want to make this small protractor from scraps of wood. To use it, first set the arm at the desired angle. Rest the base on the worktable and hold the arm against the side of the blade.

3-13 No matter how the worktable is tilted side to side, the blade should always be square to the table, front to back (if you have a parallel-arm, double-parallel link, or rigid-arm saw). If this angle is off, it's probably because the blade is not properly mounted and tensioned — remount the blade so it hangs straight and is as far back in the blade clamps as it will go. Or, add some tension. The blade may also be bent. If this is the case, discard the blade and mount a new one.

PREPARING THE BLADE

Before you use a blade for the first time, it may need a little work. With the exception of precision-ground blades, most scroll saw blades are stamped or milled from thin metal sheets. As the cutting tool exits the metal, it creates a burr on one side. This burr helps the blade to cut faster. However, it also makes the kerf wider, leaves the cut surface on the burred side rougher, and causes the blade to drift toward the burred side as you work. *(SEE FIGURE 3-14.)*

In addition, all new blades have sharp back corners. While these don't affect the quality of the cut, they limit the turning radius of the blade. If you round them over, you can turn much sharper corners. *(SEE FIGURE 3-15.)*

Depending on the scroll saw operation, you may want to remove the burrs or round the corners. You can do both by *stoning* the blade — grinding it with a small sharpening stone or a hone. With the scroll saw running, hold the stone *lightly* against the flat side to remove the burrs, and against the back corners to round them. *(SEE FIGURE 3-16.)* Be careful not to let the stone contact the front of the blade; it will dull the teeth.

Note: Don't try to remove the burrs from blades larger than number 12. Larger blades often have set teeth — the teeth are bent alternately left and right, as on a hand saw. If you stone the sides of these blades, you'll remove the set and dull the teeth.

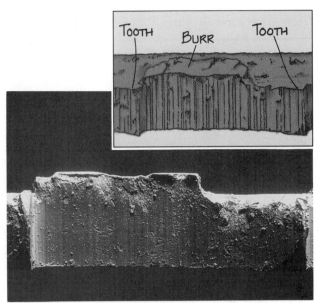

3-14 Because of the way in which most scroll saw blades are milled, they are burred on one side. These burrs (shown magnified 60 times) actually make the blade cut faster. However, because the burred side cuts more aggressively than the other, the blade cuts unevenly and tends to drift. The burrs also make the sawed surface rougher. When the burrs are removed, the blade cuts slower, but much truer and smoother. *Micrograph courtesy of George F. Vander Voort, Carpenter Technology, Reading, PA.*

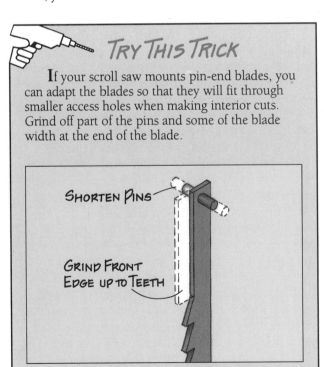

TRY THIS TRICK

If your scroll saw mounts pin-end blades, you can adapt the blades so that they will fit through smaller access holes when making interior cuts. Grind off part of the pins and some of the blade width at the end of the blade.

SHORTEN PINS

GRIND FRONT EDGE UP TO TEETH

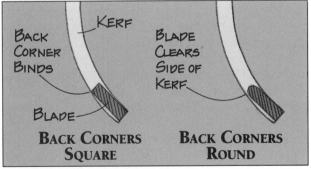

3-15 The square corners of a blade rub on the sides of the kerf when you turn a tight radius. This prevents you from cutting tight corners and creates more friction. The blade heats up in the cut, and the excess heat shortens its life. By rounding the back corners, you can cut smaller, tighter curves. The blade will stay cooler and last longer.

3-16 To remove the burrs from a blade, hold a small sharpening stone against one side of the blade while the scroll saw is running. Use a scrap of wood to back up the blade and keep it from bowing. Wait a few seconds, then reposition the stone and wood scrap and treat the other side of the blade. (You must stone both sides because you can't know which side is burred without inspecting the blade under a microscope.) To round the back of a blade, hold the stone against the back corners. Be careful not to stone the front corners — you'll dull the teeth. **Note:** Mail-order woodworking suppliers sell small stones for dressing band saw blades — these are ideal for scroll saw blades, too.

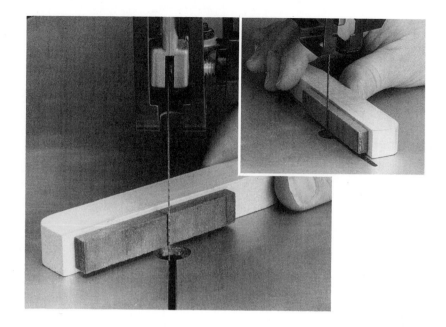

MAINTENANCE

The care required for each scroll saw depends on its design, but there are a few critical maintenance chores that must be performed on all machines.

CLEANING

Most importantly, keep your scroll saw as clean as possible. Sawdust is detrimental for several reasons:

■ It's a mild abrasive. Tiny mineral deposits in the cell walls of the wood fibers, called *extractives,* wear away metal surfaces just like sandpaper. If you allow fine sawdust to build up, it will penetrate pivots, bushings, and bearings, abrading the surfaces of the moving parts.

■ It prevents the blade clamps from getting a good grip on plain-end blades. The blades may slip when you tension them, or when you start to cut with them.

■ It interferes with electrical connections. If it builds up inside switches and other controls, it could prevent the saw from operating.

Brush the sawdust from the scroll saw as you work — this will prevent it from building up. Each time you change blades, blow the sawdust out of the blade clamps. Clean the saw before you put it away, and if you're not going to use the saw for a long time, cover it to keep dust off.

LUBRICATION

Like most of the power tools made today, modern scroll saws require little oil or grease. However, there are a few components that will benefit from occasional lubrication:

■ Wax the worktable when you first set up your scroll saw, and every few months after that — this helps the work to glide across the table surface. Apply a thin, even coat of paste wax, then *buff thoroughly.* (If the wax isn't buffed, it will do more harm than good.)

■ Apply a small amount of silicone or graphite to the pivots at the ends of the arms where the blade clamps are mounted, as well as to the pivots on both ends of the pitman arm. (*SEE FIGURE 3-17.*) You can also use 10W oil, but it should be applied very sparingly — no more than a single drop to each pivot — or it will mix with sawdust to create a thick gunk.

■ If your saw is equipped with a blower, the air pump seal may need a drop or two of oil once or twice a year. Oil keeps the seal in good working condition; without it, the seal would dry up and begin to leak, making the blower less effective.

■ If the arms pivot on bronze bushings, you may want to apply a thin coat of lithium grease to them every one or two years. Most bronze bushings are oil-impregnated and therefore self-lubricating. However, for the bronze to release the oil, it must first get hot. In other machines, the friction from rotary motion heats the bronze bushings sufficiently to do this. But the scroll saw's reciprocating motion causes less friction and the moving parts remain relatively cool. The oil is never released, and the bushings wear out from lack of lubrication. A little grease will prevent this.

Inspect the pivots and the other connections between the moving parts from time to time to be sure they move freely and they are not worn. In a reciprocating machine, it's extremely important that the pivots are neither too tight nor too loose. Tight parts will cause extra wear and tear; loose parts increase the amount of vibration.

3-17 Lubricate the blade clamp pivots *sparingly.* This helps the scroll saw to run more smoothly and prevents wear. Use graphite or silicone, and be very careful not to get any lubricant on the blade clamp jaws — this may cause the blades to slip in their clamps. If you do get a lubricant on the clamp surfaces, clean them with alcohol or acetone.

TUNING UP A SCROLL SAW

You can improve the performance of an older scroll saw (or an inexpensive one) significantly by polishing a few rough surfaces, making some design changes, and adding user-friendly accessories. Here are a few suggestions.

1 **Grind and polish the surface** of the worktable to make it as flat and smooth as possible. Affix sheets of aluminum oxide sandpaper to a large, flat sheet of glass, and rub the table back and forth on the abrasive. Work your way from 100 grit to 220 or higher — the smoother the surface, the more easily the workpiece will slide across the table. This, in turn, will make it easier to control the cuts. **Note:** *Don't* use power sanders; you may gouge the surface of the table.

(continued) ▷

TUNING UP A SCROLL SAW — CONTINUED

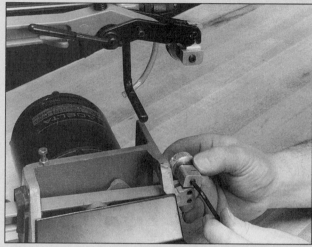

2   **By extending the saw slot in** the worktable as far forward as possible, you make it easier to thread the blade through access holes when making interior cuts. Cut the slot with a saber saw and a metal-cutting blade. Or, use two or three hacksaw blades taped together. Stop just before you reach the trunnion. Bevel the edges of the slot with a file to remove any sharp corners.

3   **Replace the machine's** standard blade clamps with quick-release clamps, if these are available for your saw. Quick-release clamps make it possible to change blades with your fingers — you don't have to keep a wrench or a key handy. See *WHERE TO FIND IT* on page 22 for sources.

4   **If your scroll saw doesn't** have a blower, install a blower kit. You can also improve the present blower system by replacing the fixed nozzle with a length of flexible coolant hose — this will allow you to direct the air where you need it. Make a metal tip for the hose from a piece of tubing, flattening the end to increase the air velocity as it exits the tube. Re-route the air from the bellows through the flexible hose. If you need more air pressure, use an air compressor instead of the bellows.

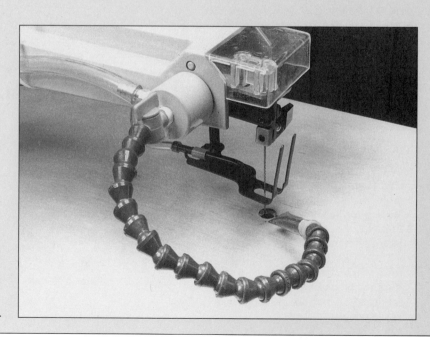

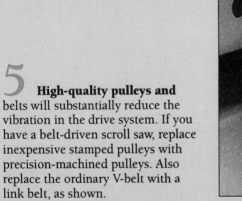

5 **High-quality pulleys and** belts will substantially reduce the vibration in the drive system. If you have a belt-driven scroll saw, replace inexpensive stamped pulleys with precision-machined pulleys. Also replace the ordinary V-belt with a link belt, as shown.

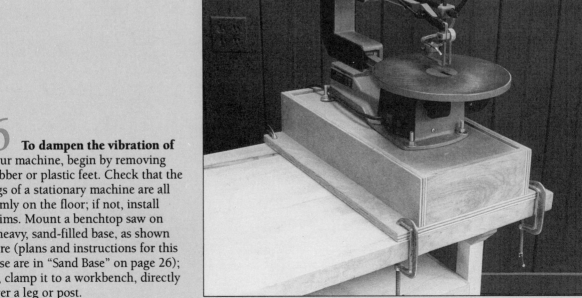

6 **To dampen the vibration of** your machine, begin by removing rubber or plastic feet. Check that the legs of a stationary machine are all firmly on the floor; if not, install shims. Mount a benchtop saw on a heavy, sand-filled base, as shown here (plans and instructions for this base are in "Sand Base" on page 26); or, clamp it to a workbench, directly over a leg or post.

4

SCROLL SAW KNOW-HOW

Of all the power saws, the scroll saw is the simplest and safest to use. There is no fence or miter gauge to set up; to start cutting, you just feed the wood into the blade. The blade cuts slowly, making it relatively easy to follow the pattern line. You don't have to worry about kickback; although the workpiece may be lifted off the table, it will not be thrown back at you. And if your fingers stray too close to the blade, the result is likely to be a minor scrape rather than a nasty accident.

However, there are some tricks and tips that will help you avoid frustrating goofs. You should know which materials are good for scroll work, how to plan both interior and exterior cuts, where to begin and end cuts, how fast to feed the work, and how to turn corners. Even though the scroll saw is a simple machine, it takes a knack to use it proficiently.

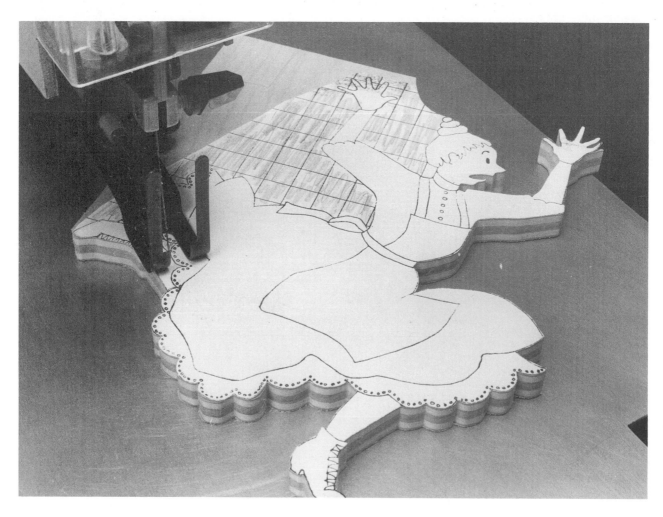

CHOOSING MATERIALS

Although the scroll saw will cut a wide variety of substances, most scroll work is done with wood or wood products — hardwood, softwood, plywood, and particleboard. Within each of these categories, some materials are better suited to a scroll saw than others. Knowing which materials work best helps ensure the success of your project.

HARDWOOD AND SOFTWOOD

When working with solid woods, you'll find that although softwoods cut faster than hardwoods, you can get good results with both materials, provided the grain pattern is small and relatively uniform. Close-grained woods such as white pine, basswood, and poplar work best, followed by medium-grained woods such as maple, cherry, birch, and beech. If you can, avoid open-grained woods such as oak, ash, walnut, and mahogany; these split more frequently than woods with closer grains, especially when you're sawing small details. (SEE FIGURE 4-1.)

Also choose clear, straight-grained wood. Knots, burls, and similar defects in the grain are much harder and denser than the surrounding wood. Not only are these defects more difficult to cut, they may *deflect* a slender scroll saw blade. (SEE FIGURE 4-2.) The blade tends to wander away from the pattern line or to cup or bow in the wood. Either way, the cut will be ruined.

You may experience the same problems when sawing wood species with pronounced growth rings, such as yellow pine, cedar, and redwood. In these woods, the dark parts of the annual rings (the *summerwood*) are much denser than the lighter portions (the *springwood*). The blade may be deflected by the dense summerwood and follow the softer springwood. (AGAIN, SEE FIGURE 4-2.)

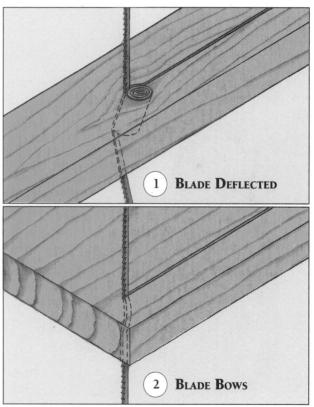

1 BLADE DEFLECTED

2 BLADE BOWS

4-1 **When sawing extremely** detailed patterns, choose close-grained woods, such as *white pine* (1). Medium-grained woods, such as *cherry* (2), may also do well. But the more open the grain, the more likely the wood is to split. Note that part of the detail on the open-grained *oak* (3) has fallen away.

4-2 **Because a scroll saw blade is** so flexible, it can be easily deflected — even when mounted and tensioned. As you cut, it tends to follow the softest part of the wood. Consequently, the blade may be pushed to one side by a hard knot (1). When cutting yellow pine and other woods with dense summerwood, the blade may cup or bow to follow the annual rings (2).

PLYWOOD AND PARTICLEBOARD

Plywood was invented in the nineteenth century especially for scroll work. Solid wood has a tendency to split along the grain, and complex wooden shapes have many weak points where the grain runs across an appendage. *(SEE FIGURE 4-3.)* Plywood, however, has no such weaknesses since it consists of several layers of wood, and the grain of each layer is perpendicular to the adjoining layers. For this reason, plywood was used extensively to make delicate scroll-sawed decorations for Victorian furniture.

The woodworking industries quickly found other uses for plywood, and they developed products for cabinetmaking and construction. Today, of the dozens of types of plywood, only a few are suitable for scroll work. If you wish to cut an intricate pattern in plywood, your best choice is *hardwood* plywood, grade A-2 or 1-2. If you use *softwood* plywood, look for grade N-B or A-B. Avoid all construction-grade plywood.

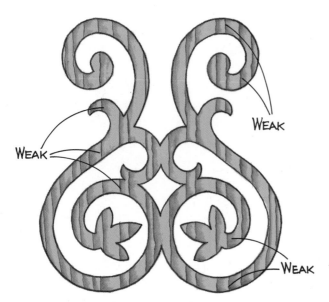

4-3 When you cut a complex pattern from solid wood, there are likely to be many weak spots. Wherever the wood grain runs across a bridge or an appendage, that portion will tend to split or break off. Portions where the grain runs parallel to the length will be stronger, but the only way to make all of the parts of the pattern equally strong is to use a cabinet-grade plywood.

FOR BEST RESULTS

Use *Baltic birch* or *Apple-ply* plywood for scroll work. The quality of these products is much higher than that of ordinary cabinet-grade plywood. The layers are uniform in color and thickness, and there are few, if any, voids.

You can also use particleboard for some scroll work. It has considerably less strength than wood or plywood, so it isn't suitable for delicate work. However, it will serve for large or simple patterns. Once again, avoid construction-grade materials; use *medium-density fiberboard* (MDF). This is made from extremely fine particles, so it has a smooth, uniform texture and is relatively soft.

FOR YOUR INFORMATION

The urea-formaldehyde glue used to bond plywood and particleboard is fairly abrasive. Consequently, these materials will dull scroll saw blades much faster than solid wood.

MAKING A CUT

SAFETY CONCERNS

Although the scroll saw is safer than other power saws, it can still break a finger or take a bite out of you if you're not careful. Follow these commonsense rules of thumb to stay out of danger.

■ Keep your hands and fingers several inches away from the blade and arms at all times. If the blade breaks, it could stab you. Your fingers may be pinched under the upper arm, especially when sawing thick stock. If you need to cut an extremely small workpiece, mount it on a thin scrap of plywood or posterboard with double-faced carpet tape, then saw both the workpiece and the scrap. *(SEE FIGURE 4-4.)*

■ Use a *foot switch* to turn the power on and off. As described in "Scroll Saw Accessories" on page 22, this lets you use both hands to control the work at all times. *(SEE FIGURE 4-5.)*

■ Whenever practical, use the hold-down to help keep the work from lifting off the worktable. Always apply constant downward pressure as you cut to keep the work firmly against the table surface.

■ Make sure there is enough light to see the work clearly — mount a tension lamp or a worklight on the scroll saw. Lamps with magnifying lenses (shown in *FIGURE 2-12* on page 24) are doubly useful.

■ Get comfortable. Because a scroll saw cuts slowly, even simple tasks may require lots of time. To make this time pass as pleasantly as possible, mount the saw so the worktable is at chest level — you shouldn't have to stoop down to see what you're cutting. For long sawing sessions, sit on a *tall* stool, rather than a chair or a short stool. This makes it easier to get up and walk around the machine when maneuvering large boards or changing the tension.

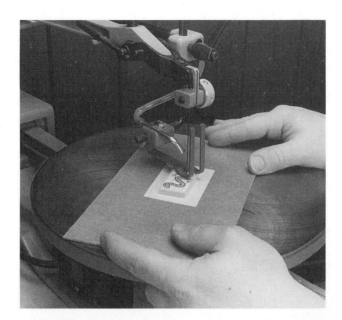

4-4 To saw a small workpiece, attach it to a large, thin scrap of plywood or posterboard with carpet tape. Cut both the scrap and the work, carefully peel the scrap from the completed work, and discard the tape. This technique not only keeps your hands out of danger, but also helps you to see what you're cutting. If you try to saw a small workpiece in the normal manner, your fingers may hide the pattern lines. **Note:** When cutting small, delicate patterns, you may want to use spray adhesive or rubber cement to adhere the workpiece to the scrap, rather than carpet tape. Carpet tape has a ferocious grip; the work may break when you try to peel it off the scrap.

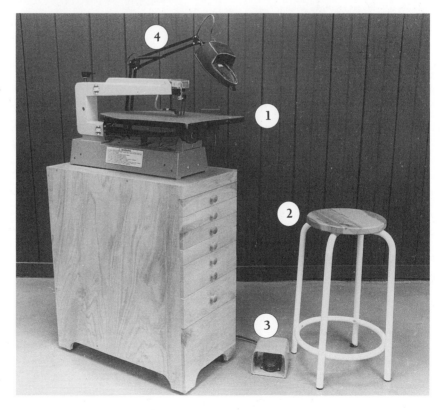

4-5 This shows a safe, comfortable scroll saw setup. The scroll saw worktable is at *chest height* (1) so you don't have to work hunched over, and there is a *tall stool* (2) to sit on. This lets you sit down for most of the sawing session, but you can stand easily to move around the saw when necessary. A *foot switch* (3) turns the saw on and off so you can keep both hands on the work. The switch is shielded to prevent you from accidentally stepping on it and turning on the machine. The worktable is brightly lit by a *tension lamp* (4). This lamp has a magnifying lens to help you see small workpieces and intricate patterns clearly.

BASIC SCROLL-WORK TECHNIQUE

No matter what sort of operation you are performing on a scroll saw, a few basic considerations always apply.

■ Adjust the hold-down so it applies enough pressure to keep the wood on the table, but not so much that it prevents you from feeding the wood into the blade. (SEE FIGURE 4-6.)

■ Before cutting good wood, turn on the saw and make sure the upper arm isn't hitting anything; if necessary, also make a test cut to check that the blade is properly mounted and tensioned.

■ When working with solid wood, plywood, and particleboard, set the scroll saw to cut at high speed (1,200 to 1,800 spm). Use a slow speed (400 to 800 spm) for exceptionally thin stock, such as veneer, and for metals, plastic, and bone.

■ When cutting veneer and other extremely thin stock, back up the work with a piece of posterboard to help control feathering. Some craftsmen prefer to sandwich thin stock between two pieces of posterboard.

■ Begin cutting across the grain, if possible. It will be easier to start the cut and control it.

■ *The feed rate is EXTREMELY important!* Feed the work slowly, using gentle pressure. Don't feed so fast that the blade bows backwards. (SEE FIGURE 4-7.) Let the saw cut the wood at its own rate.

■ The feed rate also affects the smoothness of the cut. For the smoothest possible surface, feed the wood at a slow rate.

■ Don't put side pressure on the blade — this could make it bow sideways. Carefully feed the wood so the workpiece presses against the teeth only.

CUTTING A PROFILE

When sawing a two-dimensional profile, follow these rules of thumb:

■ Begin cutting at a point or a corner in the layout, if possible, so you can saw long, straight edges and gently curved edges in a single cut. Wherever two cuts meet along an edge, there is likely to be a notice-

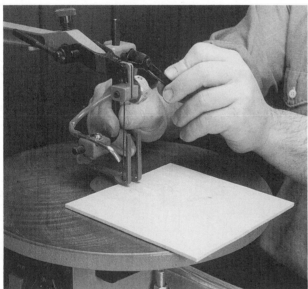

4-6 The method for adjusting the hold-down depends on the scroll saw's particular design. On most machines, you let the hold-down drop until it touches the wood, then lower it another 1/8 to 1/4 inch so the hold-down foot flexes slightly. You should be able to slide the work around under the hold-down easily. **Note:** Dress the hold-downs on new saws, rounding over the edges with a file. The sharp edges and burrs left by the manufacturing process may mar your work.

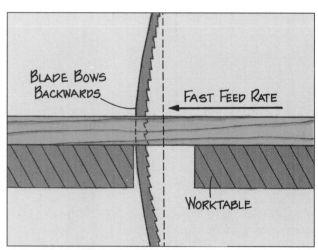

4-7 Don't feed the work too fast — remember, the scroll saw cuts much more slowly than other power saws. If you force the stock into the blade, the blade will bow, bending backwards. If you continue cutting with the blade bowed, you'll find it difficult to control the cut. Stop feeding the wood for a minute, let the blade "catch up" and straighten out, then continue, feeding more slowly.

able step or bump rather than a smooth transition. (*See Figure 4-8.*) When cuts meet at points and corners, there are no noticeable steps.

■ If you have to make two cuts meet in the middle of a line, use the saw blade as a file to nibble away any steps or bumps. This will smooth out the transition. (*See Figure 4-9.*)

■ When making a straight cut with an ordinary fret blade, you probably will find that the blade drifts to one side. Compensate for this by feeding the wood at a slight angle. (*See Figure 4-10.*)

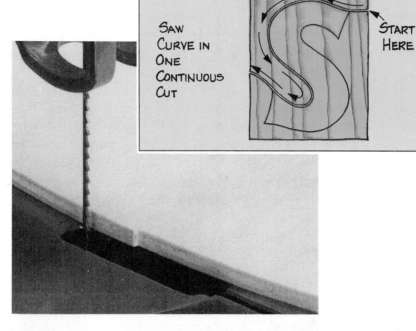

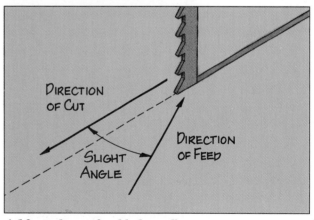

4-8 Whenever you can, start cutting at a point or corner in a layout. If you start cutting in the middle of a line or a curve, you must make a second cut to complete that portion of the design. It's difficult to make two cuts meet perfectly in the middle of a line; the result is likely to be a step or a bump in the sawed edge.

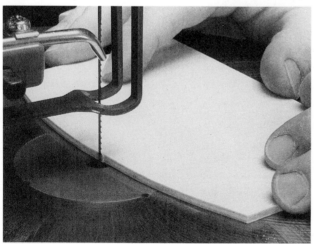

4-9 You can *nibble* away stock with a scroll saw blade, using the teeth like a tiny rasp or file. Gently press the edge of the stock against the teeth, moving it sideways as the teeth nibble the wood. This technique is very handy for smoothing over steps and bumps where two cuts meet. You can also use it to clean out tight corners.

4-10 Ordinary fret blades will drift to one side when you try to cut a straight line. This is because the teeth are not milled precisely, and they cut more aggressively on one side than the other. To compensate, feed the wood at a slight angle, or use precision-ground blades. Because the teeth on these blades are cut more accurately and with few burrs, blade drift is reduced and the cut is much easier to control.

TRY THIS TRICK

To make a perfectly straight cut on a scroll saw, use a precision-ground blade or a spiral blade, and guide the stock with a fence. Create a temporary fence by fastening a straightedge to the worktable with carpet tape. If you use a spiral blade, you can position the fence anywhere on the worktable. For a precision-ground blade, the fence must be roughly parallel to the side of the blade. (Don't try this with an ordinary blade; it will drift too badly to use a fence.)

■ When cutting curves with blades that are larger than a number 5, don't try to make turns with radii that are too small for the blade. The blade will bind in the cuts. To cut tight outside curves with a wide blade, enlarge the kerf so the blade has room to turn. (SEE FIGURE 4-11.) To make tight inside curves, drill holes in the pattern so you don't have to cut them at all. The radius of each hole should match the radius of its curve. (SEE FIGURE 4-12.)

■ When cutting sharp corners with blades larger than a number 5, make two or more cuts. To saw an outside corner, cut past the corner, then loop around or backtrack so you can start cutting again at the corner. (SEE FIGURE 4-13.) For inside corners, saw to the corner, then make another cut to meet the first. (SEE FIGURE 4-14.)

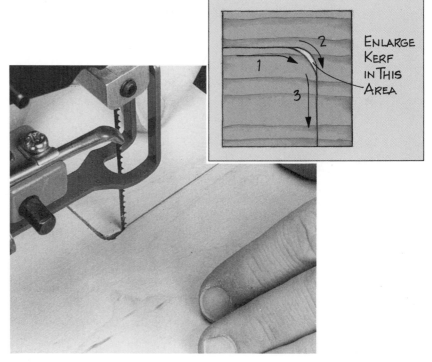

ENLARGE KERF IN THIS AREA

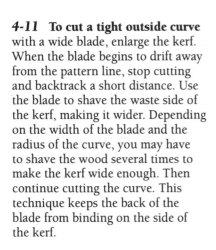

4-11 To cut a tight outside curve with a wide blade, enlarge the kerf. When the blade begins to drift away from the pattern line, stop cutting and backtrack a short distance. Use the blade to shave the waste side of the kerf, making it wider. Depending on the width of the blade and the radius of the curve, you may have to shave the wood several times to make the kerf wide enough. Then continue cutting the curve. This technique keeps the back of the blade from binding on the side of the kerf.

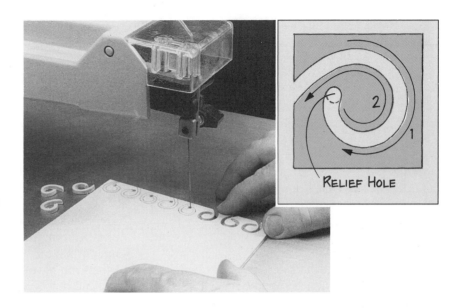

RELIEF HOLE

4-12 **To cut tight inside curves** with a blade that's too wide to make the turns, drill relief holes in the waste. The radii of the holes and the curves must match. Cut along the pattern line until you enter a hole. Turn the workpiece while the blade is inside the hole, then cut away from the hole, continuing to follow the pattern line.

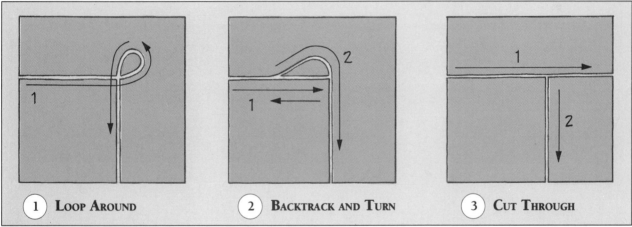

| ① LOOP AROUND | ② BACKTRACK AND TURN | ③ CUT THROUGH |

4-13 **There are three common** methods for cutting outside corners with wide blades. (1) Cut past the corner, then loop around so the blade crosses its own path at the corner, and continue cutting. (2) Cut up to the corner, backtrack a short distance, and cut away from the pattern line. Curve around to meet the cut at the corner and con-tinue cutting. (3) Cut past the corner to the cutside edge of the workpiece. Remove the scrap, then start cutting again at the corner.

4-14 **There are two ways to cut** sharp inside corners with wide blades. (1) Saw to the corner, cutting along one of the converging pattern lines. Stop at the corner, then back-track completely out of the cut. Start again, following the second pattern line until you meet the first at the corner. (2) Saw to the corner along one line, then backtrack a short dis-tance. Turn around in the waste, and cut along the second line until you exit the stock. Finish by making a third cut along the second line to the corner.

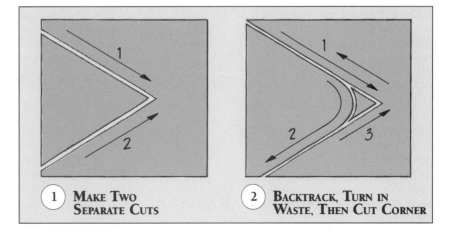

| ① MAKE TWO SEPARATE CUTS | ② BACKTRACK, TURN IN WASTE, THEN CUT CORNER |

■ By using narrow blades (number 5 or smaller), you can cut tight curves or corners without backtracking and making additional cuts — the blade will follow almost any pattern line, no matter how small the curves. In fact, with a little practice, you can make *zero-radius turns* with narrow blades, spinning the stock around the blade to cut a corner. (SEE FIGURE 4-15.)

■ To cut duplicate patterns, stack the workpieces face to face and hold the stack together with carpet tape. Trace the pattern on the top piece in the stack, then cut the entire stack at once. Take the pieces apart and discard the tape.

MAKING INTERIOR CUTS

An interior cut is one that doesn't begin or end at the perimeter of the workpiece. You begin somewhere in the middle of the stock and cut away waste from the interior, without ever sawing through to an edge or end. An example would be cutting the center of an "O."

To begin an interior cut, you must first drill a hole in the stock to start the blade. (SEE FIGURE 4-16.) This hole, or *saw gate,* should be large enough to thread the blade through the wood. If the blade has plain ends, the hole should be larger in diameter than the blade is wide; if it has pin ends, the hole should be larger than the pin is long.

Release one end of the blade from its clamp and thread it through the saw gate in the workpiece. (SEE FIGURE 4-17.) Mount the blade in the clamp again, tension the blade, and adjust the hold-down. Begin cutting out from the saw gate to the pattern line. Cut the interior pattern, removing bits of waste as you work. When you have finished cutting the pattern, release one end of the blade from its clamp and pull the blade from the cutout.

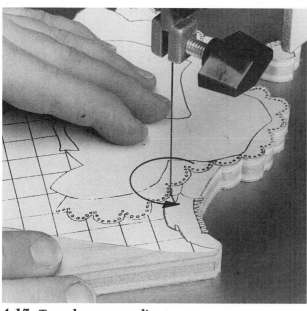

4-15 To make a *zero-radius turn,* use a narrow blade (number 5 or smaller). Cut up to a point or a corner in the pattern, then slowly spin the workpiece around the blade without feeding the stock into the teeth. Be careful not to turn the stock so fast that the blade twists; let the teeth nibble away at the side of the kerf as you turn. When you have turned the stock as far as necessary, start cutting again. Zero-radius turns require some practice, so make some test cuts in scrap wood before you cut good stock.

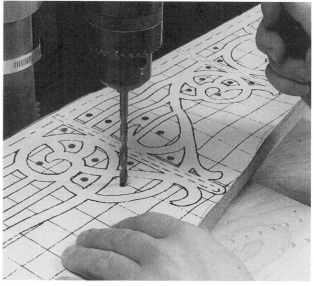

4-16 To begin an interior cut, first drill a *saw gate* (starter hole for the blade). If possible, drill the saw gate in the waste. If there isn't a great deal of room for a saw gate, drill it in a curve in the pattern. Make the hole the same radius as the curve, with the circumference touching the pattern line. If you can't locate the saw gate in the waste, drill it right on the pattern line. Make as small a hole as possible, and use a blade small enough to fit through it. Before you drill, back up the stock with a scrap to reduce tear-out when the drill exits the wood. Sand off any splinters.

4-17 The procedure for threading a blade through a saw gate depends on the design of the saw. On most scroll saws, you must release the *top* end of the blade from the top blade clamp and tilt the blade forward in the table slot. Place the workpiece over the blade so the free end pokes through the hole, push the workpiece back so the blade is vertical again, and fasten the blade in the top clamp. Some Excalibur saws and the "Shop-Made Scroll Saw" on page 74 have a feature called a *top arm lift* that simplifies this process; you release the *bottom* end of the blade, lift the top arm (with the blade attached), and poke the blade through the saw gate from the top.

BEVEL CUTTING

To cut a beveled edge with a scroll saw, tilt the table to the proper angle and begin cutting. Although this sounds simple enough, it requires careful planning. You must make all of the cuts in the *same direction* — clockwise or counterclockwise — around the perimeter of the pattern. (*SEE FIGURES 4-18 AND 4-19.*) This is necessary for both interior and outside cuts.

The most obvious application for this technique is cutting chamfers and scallops on the edges of workpieces. You can also use it to make incised signs and patterns, spirals and concentric shapes, and relieved or recessed patterns. (*SEE FIGURE 4-20.*)

> ## TRY THIS TRICK
> **T**o make a thoroughly puzzling puzzle, cut out the pieces on a bevel. To work the puzzle, not only must you arrange the pieces so they fit together, you must also assemble them in the proper order.

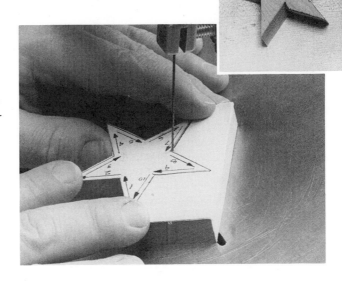

4-18 To cut a consistent bevel along a pattern, you must make all the cuts in the same direction around the perimeter of the pattern. On this star pattern, for example, the sides must be beveled so that the bottom surface will be larger than the top. To do this, the table is tilted to the left and the cuts proceed clockwise. If you reverse directions and cut a portion of the pattern counterclockwise, that portion will be beveled in the opposite direction (making the bottom surface smaller than the top), as shown on the left in the inset photo.

4-19 Cutting sharp inside corners
on a bevel is tricky — you *must*
make a zero-radius turn to keep the
cut moving in the proper direction.
If you make two separate cuts that
meet at an inside corner, one of two
things will happen: (1) The cuts will
meet on one surface, but not on the
other, as shown on the *top* in the
inset photo, or (2) the cuts will meet
on one surface, but they will cross
each other on the other, as shown in
the *middle*. (3) If you make a zero-
radius turn, the corner will be sharp
on one surface and rounded on the
other, as shown on the *bottom*.

4-20 These three projects were
all made by bevel-cutting on a scroll
saw. The basket (*left*) is made with a
long spiral cut at a 5-degree bevel.
When you lift the outer edges of the
beveled spiral, the workpiece falls
into a cone shape. The interiors of
the letters on the sign (*middle*) are
cut out on a 30-degree bevel to look
as if they were incised with a V-shaped
chisel. The outlines of the decorative
scene (*right*) are cut on a 3-degree
bevel. When the shapes in the fore-
ground are pushed forward, the
edges wedge tight against those
in the background. The result is a
pattern that appears to be carved
in relief.

COMPOUND CUTTING

You can create three-dimensional shapes on the scroll saw by making compound cuts. This involves cutting the same workpiece *twice*, making the second cut on a plane that's 90 degrees from the first. Mark patterns on two adjacent surfaces of the wood. Cut the first pattern, and save the scrap. (*SEE FIGURE 4-21.*) Tape the scrap back on the workpiece, then cut the second pattern. (*SEE FIGURE 4-22.*) When you remove the tape and the scrap, the workpiece will appear to be sculpted. (*SEE FIGURE 4-23.*)

This technique works for both outside and interior cuts. (*SEE FIGURE 4-24.*) You can use it to create small wooden sculptures, ornaments, chess pieces, and miniature boxes. (*SEE FIGURE 4-25.*)

4-21 To make a compound cut, first mark patterns on two adjacent surfaces of the workpiece. (Each pattern should be 90 degrees from the other.) Cut one pattern, saving the scrap. If possible, cut the pattern in a single cut, making zero-radius turns at the corners — this will keep the scrap in one piece.

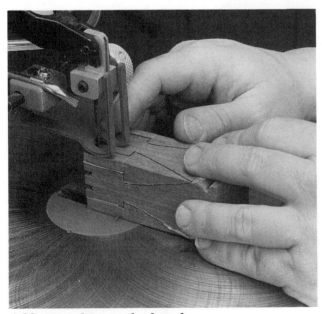

4-22 Tape the scrap back to the workpiece using double-faced carpet tape. This will make the stock rectangular again. Rotate the wood 90 degrees so the second pattern faces up, and cut it.

4-23 When you remove the scrap and discard the tape, the workpiece will have a three-dimensional shape. The rook chess piece shown was created using the same pattern for both cuts, so its shape is symmetrical. However, you can use two *different* patterns to make more-complex shapes. The knight, for example, required different patterns for the front and the side profiles.

4-24 You can also make compound *interior* cuts. After marking two adjacent patterns, drill two saw gates — each saw gate will be 90 degrees from the other. Cut the first pattern, turn the stock 90 degrees, and cut the second. You don't have to tape the scrap back to the workpiece for the second cut since the stock remains rectangular.

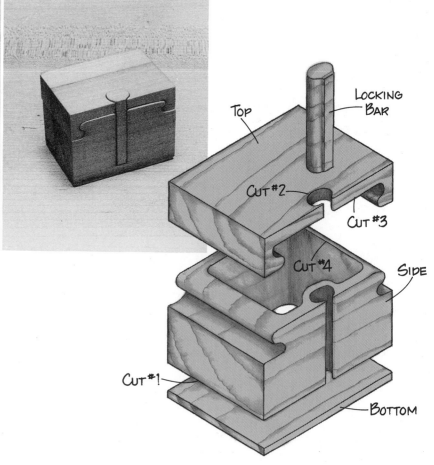

4-25 Use a variation of the compound cutting technique to create a small box from a single piece of wood. You can make many different types of boxes, both simple and complex, by carefully planning the cuts to create the box parts. For example, to make the box shown, first cut the bottom (1) free from the stock. Next, cut the locking bar (2), followed by the sliding top (3) and the box sides (4). Glue the sides to the bottom, slide the top over the sides, and drop the locking bar in place.

5

SPECIAL SCROLL SAW APPLICATIONS

Several special woodworking techniques rely heavily on the scroll saw, the most obvious of which is *pattern work* — sawing complex shapes in wood. The oldest and probably the best known type of pattern work is fretwork — intricate, lacelike designs that pierce the wood.

The scroll saw is also used in *marquetry* and *intarsia*. In both of these decorative techniques, tiny pieces of wood or veneer from different species are fitted together, creating colorful patterns and pictures. These may be applied to backing boards or the flat surfaces of furniture.

You can even use a scroll saw for certain types of *wood joinery*. Properly handled, the machine cuts as fine and true as a dovetail saw, making it a good choice for dovetails, bridle joints, and similar assemblies. And because it cuts complex shapes, the scroll saw is also a good tool for coped joints.

PATTERN WORK

Several types of pattern work can be cut on a scroll saw, and they all rely on roughly the same techniques. We've discussed one type already — fretwork, the craft that gave rise to the scroll saw. (See "Choosing a Scroll Saw" on page 2.) The term *fret* originally referred to a lattice, and fretwork was an ornamental pattern of intersecting lines and straight geometrical patterns that was carved in wood. The invention of the fret saw made it possible to saw fretwork, rather than cut it with a knife, and to create curved forms as well as the traditional straight ones. Today, fretwork patterns resemble lace more than lattice.

Other popular types of pattern work include architectural gingerbread, cutout signs, pictorial silhouettes, and three-dimensional constructions. (*SEE FIGURE 5-1.*)

All of these techniques are exclusively decorative. Although pieces cut with complex designs can be used for structural parts of a project, the designs have no function other than aesthetic effect. This work may be applied to a surface, or it may be used without backing. Applied patterns are said to be *in relief;* those without backing are sometimes called *openwork.*

LAYING OUT A PATTERN

The first step in any pattern work project is to find or develop a pattern. Scroll saw patterns can be found in books, magazines, templates, and single sheets, sold through the mail and in woodworking stores. (*SEE FIGURES 5-2 AND 5-3.*)

5-1 Perhaps the best known type of decorative pattern work is *fretwork* (1) — lacelike designs such as those in the display shelves. Others include silhouettes (2), cutout signs (3), architectural gingerbread (4), and three-dimensional scenes and constructions (5), like the whirligig. In each example, the pattern is relatively intricate, the material is wood or wood products, and a scroll saw has been used. Consequently, they all rely on similar woodworking methods.

WHERE TO FIND IT

You can purchase books of scroll saw patterns through most mail-order woodworking suppliers, including Seyco and Advanced Machinery Imports Ltd. (Their addresses are listed in WHERE TO FIND IT on page 22.) Seyco also offers various sizes and styles of lettering templates for scroll-work signs. Additionally, some suppliers specialize in patterns. Nelson Designs offers patterns for novelty items, Reidle Products has fretwork patterns, and Scroller has developed unique three-dimensional patterns. For a catalog, write:

Nelson Designs
P.O. Box 422
Dublin, NH 03444

Reidle Products
Box 58
Yuba, WI 54634

Scroller
9033 South Nashville Road
Oak Lawn, IL 60453

The editors of *Wood Magazine* regularly publish large sheets of full-size patterns. For a subscription, contact:

Wood Magazine's
  Super Scroll Saw Patterns
1716 Locust Street
Des Moines, IA 50309

5-3 You can purchase durable plastic lettering templates for sign making, in different sizes and typefaces. Use the templates to lay out letters directly on the wood or to make paper patterns. First draw a straight line on the surface to help align the letters. Position the first letter on the line and trace around it. Position the second letter next to the first — some templates include a device to help space the letters evenly. Continue until you have laid out the entire sign.

5-2 There is a wide variety of commercial scroll saw patterns available for fretwork, gingerbread, silhouettes, and three-dimensional scenes. Some must be photocopied from the pages of books; others are printed on loose sheets that can be mounted on the wood surface. Some are full-size; others need to be enlarged. Some are shaded so you know what to cut away; others are simple line drawings. Some indicate the grain direction to help orient the pattern when you transfer it to the wood surface; others don't. In short, some require more planning and preparation than others. When buying patterns, consider the work you must do just to get the project to the point where you can begin cutting.

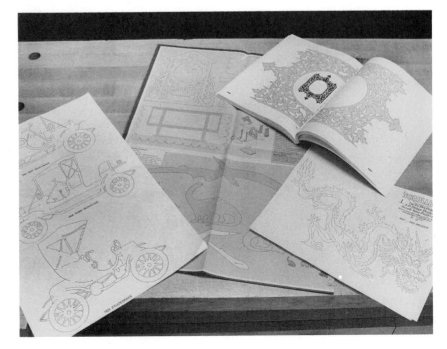

You can also devise your own patterns. Use pictures clipped from magazines, photographs, logos, lettering templates — almost any two-dimensional design will do, provided it has a clear, recognizable outline. If you use a picture or a photo, it should be in sharp focus and have high contrast to make the important details stand out. (SEE FIGURE 5-4.) You must also be able to transfer or attach the design to the wood surface.

When developing patterns for openwork, remember that all the parts must be connected so that the interior pieces stay in place. The easiest way to make these connections is to plan unobtrusive *bridges* wherever needed to connect an interior piece to the rest of the pattern. (SEE FIGURE 5-5.)

If the pattern needs to be sized, there are several techniques you might use. One of the simplest uses a photocopy machine with the capability to enlarge and reduce. Most copying services have these machines, although many copiers are limited to enlarging and reducing by a few specific percentages. Also, photocopiers often distort a pattern slightly when they change its size.

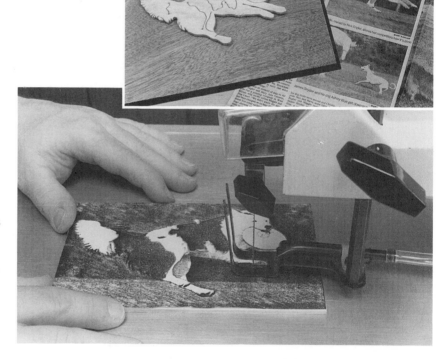

5-4 You can use photos and pictures for patterns when sawing silhouettes or scenes. Carefully consider what parts you will cut away. Before cutting good wood on the scroll saw, you may want to experiment by cutting out paper silhouettes with scissors to see how the completed pattern will look. When you've decided where to saw, make a photocopy of the subject and attach it to the wood surface with spray adhesive. Cut away the waste, then peel the remains of the photocopy off the wood.

5-5 When you draw an openwork pattern that has interior parts, you must connect these parts with slender *bridges* or they'll fall away. For example, to cut out this "OPEN" sign, you couldn't sever the bridges that connect the center of the "O" and the "P" to the rest of the sign.

A *pantograph* offers more precision, although it requires more work. With this drafting tool, you trace a pattern and draw a scaled duplicate 125 to 1,000 percent larger than the original. *(SEE FIGURE 5-6.)* If you don't have a pantograph, you can always use the traditional *squares method*. Draw a small grid over the pattern (if there isn't a grid already), and a scaled-up grid on a separate sheet of paper. Wherever a pattern line intersects a line on the smaller grid, make a corresponding dot on the larger one. Then connect the dots. *(SEE FIGURE 5-7.)*

When laying out the pattern, you can *attach* it to the wood surface, *transfer* the pattern from the paper to the surface, or *trace* the pattern on the surface.

■ To attach a paper pattern, use rubber cement or spray adhesive. Spread the cement or adhesive on the

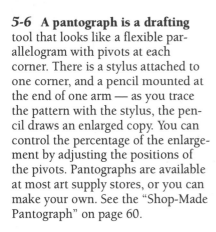

5-6 A pantograph is a drafting tool that looks like a flexible parallelogram with pivots at each corner. There is a stylus attached to one corner, and a pencil mounted at the end of one arm — as you trace the pattern with the stylus, the pencil draws an enlarged copy. You can control the percentage of the enlargement by adjusting the positions of the pivots. Pantographs are available at most art supply stores, or you can make your own. See the "Shop-Made Pantograph" on page 60.

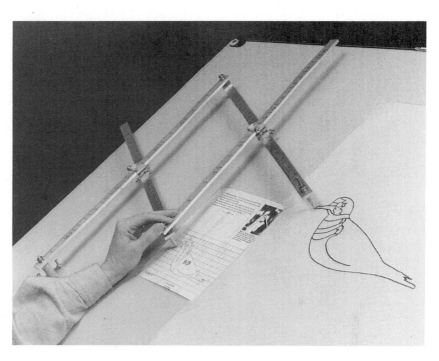

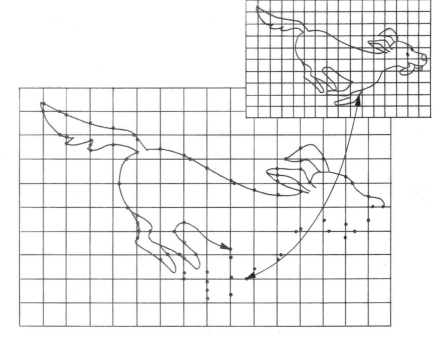

5-7 To enlarge a pattern using the squares method, draw a grid of ¹/₄-inch squares over it. Decide how large you want to make the pattern, and draw a scaled-up grid on a separate sheet of paper. For example, if you want to enlarge the pattern three times (300 percent), draw a grid of ³/₄-inch squares — 3 times ¹/₄ equals ³/₄. There should be exactly as many horizontal and vertical lines on the large grid as on the small one. To help keep track, you may want to number the lines. Wherever a pattern line meets one of the smaller grid lines, make a dot on the corresponding position on the larger grid. Then connect the dots.

paper; if you apply it to the wood, the pattern will be more difficult to remove and the chemical residue may interfere with the finish. Let the pattern dry until tacky, then stick it to the surface.

■ To transfer a pattern, tape carbon paper to the underside of the paper sheet, lay the sheet on the wood, and trace the pattern lines with a ballpoint pen. Or, lay the pattern (without the carbon paper) on the wood and trace the lines with a *pounce wheel.* (*SEE FIGURE 5-8.*) If you make a photocopy of the pattern, you can transfer the copy by laying it face down on the wood and ironing it. (*SEE FIGURE 5-9.*)

■ To trace a pattern or a template, use a color of pencil that stands out clearly from the wood. Some

craftsmen spin the pencil between their fingers as they trace the lines — this keeps the tip sharp so that the line doesn't broaden.

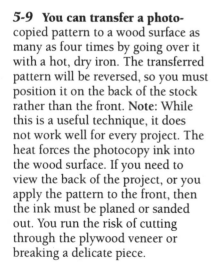

TRY THIS TRICK

If you need to use a paper pattern over and over again, turn it into a durable plastic template by mounting the paper on a piece of ⅛-inch-thick acrylic. Cut out the pattern on the scroll saw at a slow speed, using a blade designed to cut plastic. Clean up any rough edges with a file.

5-8 Use a star wheel or a *pounce* *wheel* to transfer paper patterns. Simply roll the wheel along the pattern lines, pressing hard enough to force the points on the wheel through the paper and into the wood. If you have trouble seeing the indentations in the wood after you remove the pattern, dust the wood with powdered blue chalk (the kind used for snap lines). **Note:** Don't use red or yellow chalk. These may stain the wood.

5-9 You can transfer a photo-copied pattern to a wood surface as many as four times by going over it with a hot, dry iron. The transferred pattern will be reversed, so you must position it on the back of the stock rather than the front. **Note:** While this is a useful technique, it does not work well for every project. The heat forces the photocopy ink into the wood surface. If you need to view the back of the project, or you apply the pattern to the front, then the ink must be planed or sanded out. You run the risk of cutting through the plywood veneer or breaking a delicate piece.

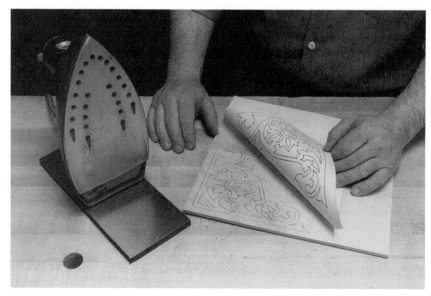

Whatever method you use, remember that solid wood is strongest along the wood grain. As you lay out the pattern, orient it so the longest portions of the design are parallel to the grain direction. *(SEE FIGURE 5-10.)* If the pattern has extensions and appendages that go off in all directions, consider cutting it from plywood instead of solid wood. Plywood is equally strong in all directions.

Once you have laid out the pattern, shade it so there's a clear difference between the areas you want to cut away and those you don't. *(SEE FIGURE 5-11.)* It's very easy to lose track of what's waste and what isn't, especially when cutting a complex pattern.

CUTTING PATTERNS

There are no special methods or tricks for cutting pattern work; use the straightforward techniques for cutting shapes discussed in "Cutting a Profile" on page 44. The only difference between sawing simple shapes and sawing a pattern is the quantity of work involved. Complex patterns can require hours of sawing.

To help the work go faster:

■ Get comfortable. Sit on a stool as you work, use a foot switch to turn the machine on and off, and attach a light to the saw stand. If the pattern is extremely intricate, use a magnifying lamp, loupe, or headband magnifier to help you see the lines.

■ Gather all your tools in one location, within arm's reach. Place the saw next to a workbench and lay out a drill, drill bits, extra saw blades, files, sandpaper, pencils, patterns, rubber cement, and all other necessary materials and accessories.

■ Develop a rhythm — an order in which you perform the necessary tasks. This is especially useful for changing blades and threading blades through saw gates. It provides mental checklists for procedures that you must repeat over and over again and helps keep you from working sloppily or unsafely.

■ Some pattern work requires that you duplicate complex designs. When this is the case, pad-saw the patterns so you can make several at one time.

■ Change blades when the feed rate seems to slow down — the blade is probably dull. Don't try to wear out a blade. Dull blades burn the surface, and they may break in the middle of a cut.

GRAIN HORIZONTAL   **GRAIN VERTICAL**

5-10 **When positioning a pattern,** remember that the wood is strongest parallel to the wood grain. Arrange the pattern to create as few weak spots as possible. For example, if the grain runs horizontally on the silhouette pattern shown, the stems and leaves of the flowers will be very weak. The pattern is much stronger when the grain runs vertically. If there will be too many weak spots no matter which way you orient your pattern, consider using plywood.

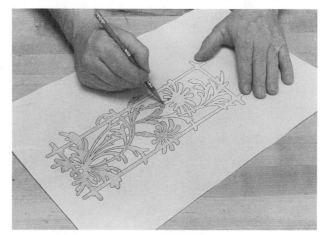

5-11 **Shade intricate patterns so** you know what to cut away and what to leave in place. (Many patterns come already shaded.) It's too easy to saw through a bridge or eliminate an important part of a design when the waste and the pattern look the same. **Note:** Don't make the shading too dark, or the blade will be hard to see.

SHOP-MADE PANTOGRAPH

Make your own pantograph from a few scraps of hardwood. Cut the parts and drill the ³/₁₆-inch-diameter holes labeled "10X" in arms A, B, C, and D. Stack the arms face to face, aligning the "10X" holes, and tape them together. Drill the remaining "X" holes. Take the stack apart and label the holes "2X," "3X," "4X," and so on, as shown in the *Arm Layout,* to note the various enlargements that you can make.

Drill the remaining ³/₁₆-inch-diameter holes at the ends of the arms. Glue the stiffener to the end of arm D and drill a hole through both parts — the diameter of the hole should match that of the mechanical pencil you intend to use in the com-

pleted pantograph. To make a clamp for the pencil, drill a ³/₁₆-inch-diameter hole through the stiffener, then open up the hole by sawing a slot from the end.

Drill holes in the fulcrum base and spacer, and glue them together. Grind a rounded point on the bolt that will serve as the stylus — don't make it too sharp, or it will tear the paper when you trace the patterns. Grind the head of the support bolt flat and polish the edges. This bolt must glide across the surface of the drawing board while holding the pantograph arms above the paper. Assemble the fulcrum, arms, and pencil with bolts, washers, stop nuts, and a knurled nut.

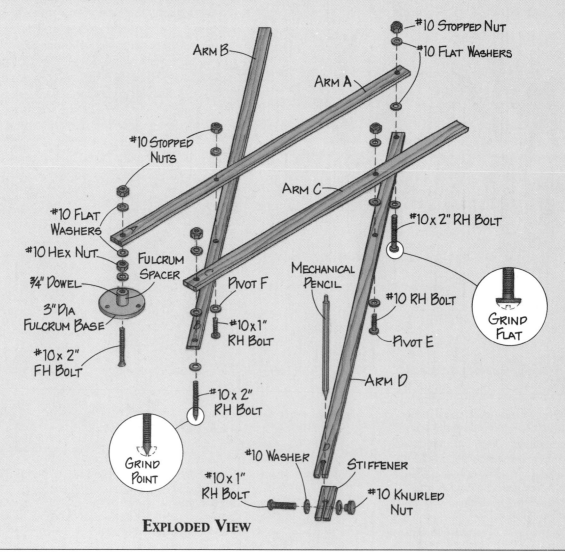

EXPLODED VIEW

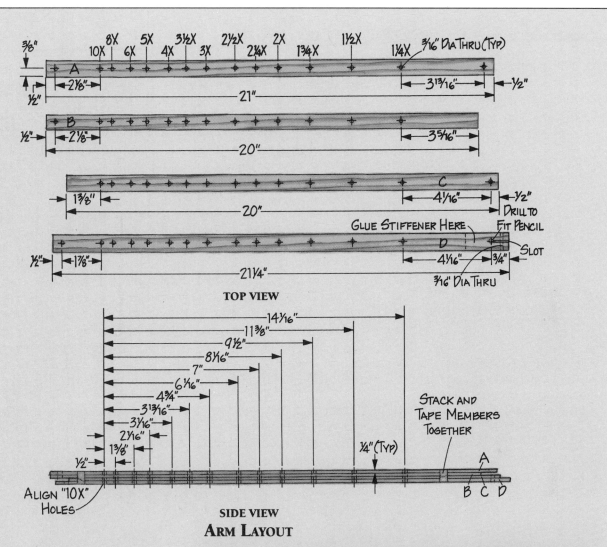

TOP VIEW

SIDE VIEW
ARM LAYOUT

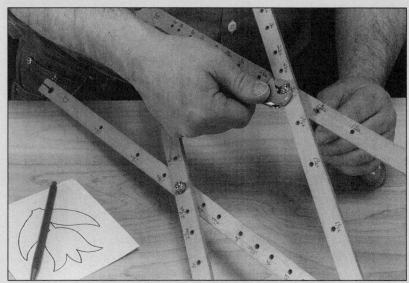

1 **To use the pantograph, first** decide how much you want to enlarge the original pattern. Locate the holes in the arms that match the enlargement percentage as closely as possible, and move the adjustable pivots — E and F — to these holes. For instance, if you want to enlarge the pattern three times, or 300 percent, move the pivots to the holes labeled "3X." All four holes (each pivot passes through two) must be labeled the same for the pantograph to work accurately. Adjust the stop nuts that hold the pivot bolts, making sure the arms move freely but with little or no slop.

(continued) ▷

SHOP-MADE PANTOGRAPH — CONTINUED

2 **Attach the fulcrum base to** the drawing surface with screws. (You can use a sheet of plywood or the top of your workbench as a drawing surface.) Tape the pattern to the surface under the stylus and a blank sheet of paper under the pencil. Roughly trace the perimeter of the pattern to make sure the pencil will stay on the paper. You may have to shift the paper, the pattern, or both.

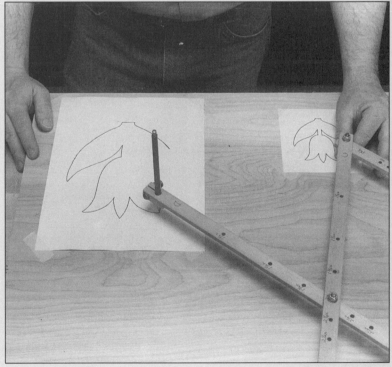

3 **Carefully trace the pattern** with the stylus, and the pencil will make an enlarged copy on the paper. If the lines in the copy are too light, or there are gaps in the lines, adjust the height of the pencil so the lead rests firmly on the paper. Advance the lead in the pencil as it wears away. When you must move the stylus from one pattern line to another, lift both the stylus and the pencil.

MARQUETRY AND INTARSIA

In *marquetry*, tiny bits of veneers are pieced together to form a pattern or a picture. Usually, several different species or colors of veneer will be used to make the design stand out. *Intarsia* is a similar art form, but the craftsman uses thicker pieces of wood. Often the pieces are of various thicknesses and the edges are shaped to give the design some depth. (*SEE FIGURE 5-12.*) Both crafts rely on many of the same scroll saw techniques.

The first step in any marquetry or intarsia project is to choose wood, selecting species for their color and how they contrast when placed next to one another. To plan the colors you will be using, you can experiment with pencils, crayons, or markers that approximate colors of the woods available to you. Make photocopies of the pattern and color them — it may take several tries to get a pleasing combination. **Note:** For some projects, you may want to use just one species of light-colored wood, such as white pine or basswood, then stain or paint the pieces.

Marquetry — If you're making a marquetry project, you must flatten the curled sheets of veneer before you cut them. Wet the veneers with a damp cloth and clamp them between two thick sheets of plywood for a week or two to dry them flat. If you're in a hurry, wipe the veneers with a damp cloth, then go over them with a hot, dry iron. Use the veneers immediately after flattening, or they'll curl up again as they absorb moisture from the air.

Stack the veneers on a piece of thick posterboard, and tape them to one another to keep them from shift-ing. (*SEE FIGURE 5-13.*) Tape another posterboard over the stack so the veneers are sandwiched between two sheets. Mount the pattern on the top posterboard.

5-13 After flattening the veneers, stack them on stiff posterboard. Tape the first veneer sheet to the poster-board with masking tape, then tape the second sheet to the first, and so on, until all the sheets are taped to one another. This will prevent the stack from shifting. Place a second posterboard over the stack and tape it down, sandwiching the veneers between the posterboards. Mount the pattern on the top posterboard with spray adhesive.

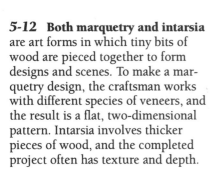

5-12 Both marquetry and intarsia are art forms in which tiny bits of wood are pieced together to form designs and scenes. To make a mar-quetry design, the craftsman works with different species of veneers, and the result is a flat, two-dimensional pattern. Intarsia involves thicker pieces of wood, and the completed project often has texture and depth.

Drill tiny saw gates where necessary, and cut the pieces of the pattern with a fine blade. (SEE FIGURE 5-14.) Sort out the veneer species or color needed for each piece and reassemble the pieces on a flat surface. Hold them together with veneer tape. (SEE FIGURE 5-15.) Attach the pattern to a backing board with contact cement, and remove the tape. (SEE FIGURE 5-16.) If necessary, fill any gaps left by the saw kerfs.

TRY THIS TRICK

Use the leftover pieces to make additional marquetry patterns — the arrangement of the colors will be different, but the designs will be the same. You can make one pattern for every sheet of veneer in the stack.

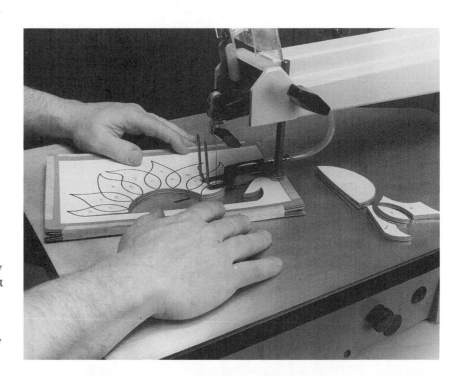

5-14 Select a blade that leaves as small a kerf as practicable. Use a number 2/0 if you're only sawing through two or three sheets of veneer, and a number 0 or 1 for thicker stacks. Drill the necessary saw gates, making them as small as possible. If you can, locate them where pattern lines intersect — they will be less noticeable. Set the saw at its slowest speed and cut the pieces of the design. Carefully label or organize the parts as you cut them so you won't get them mixed up. If any of the pieces break, save the chips.

5-15 Prepare an assembly board by spraying a piece of plywood or posterboard with adhesive. This will give it some tack so the pieces will stay put. Locate the species or the color you want for each piece, and fit the pieces back together on the assembly board. If any of the parts have broken off, include them as well; make replacements for misplaced fragments from veneer scraps. When the pattern is assembled, apply gum-backed veneer tape to hold all the parts together. Lift the completed pattern off the assembly board.

5-16 Attach the marquetry pattern (taped surface *up*) to a backing board with contact cement, in the same manner that you would attach an ordinary sheet of veneer. Wet the veneer tape with a damp cloth and carefully peel it off the pattern. If any of the veneer pieces come loose, reapply them with a thin coat of contact cement. Fill any visible saw gates or saw kerfs with stick shellac or epoxy glue. Finish sand the pattern, being careful not to sand through the veneers. Finally, apply a finish.

Intarsia — To make an intarsia design, first plane the selected woods to the desired thicknesses. Stack the boards face to face, sticking them together with double-faced carpet tape. (*SEE FIGURE 5-17.*) Mount a pattern on the top board in the stack. Drill saw gates, if needed, and cut the pieces of the design. (*SEE FIGURE 5-18.*) Carefully label each piece as you cut it.

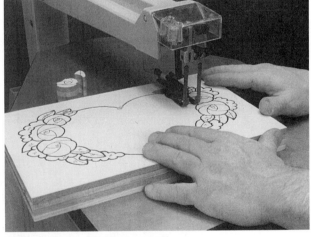

5-18 Select a blade that will leave as small a kerf as practicable. Because you're sawing thicker stock, you probably won't be able to use as fine a blade as you can for marquetry, but try not to use one larger than number 5 — this will allow you to make zero-radius turns, if need be. Drill the necessary saw gates and cut the parts. After cutting, carefully peel the layers apart and discard the tape. Organize the parts so you can fit them back together easily. If you need to label them, write on the *bottom* surfaces, especially if you plan to round over or carve the top edges.

5-17 Plane the wood you've selected to the thicknesses needed. Stack the boards face to face, holding them together with double-faced carpet tape. Using spray adhesive, mount the pattern on the top board in the stack.

From the pieces you've cut, select the species or the color you decided on previously. If you want the completed design to have some depth, round over the top edges of each piece with a drum sander. (SEE FIGURE 5-19.) Glue the pieces to a backing board. To further enhance the three-dimensional effect of the design, you may wish to carve the top surfaces of some pieces. (SEE FIGURE 5-20.)

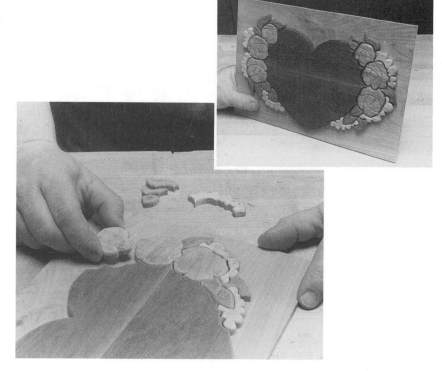

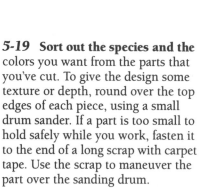

5-19 **Sort out the species and the** colors you want from the parts that you've cut. To give the design some texture or depth, round over the top edges of each piece, using a small drum sander. If a part is too small to hold safely while you work, fasten it to the end of a long scrap with carpet tape. Use the scrap to maneuver the part over the sanding drum.

5-20 **Fit together all the parts on** a flat surface, and check whether any of the elements need further sanding. Glue one part at a time to the backing board — spread an even film of white or yellow glue on the back surface and press it down on the board to get a good bond. It's not necessary to clamp the parts in place unless they are exceptionally large. Let the glue dry overnight, then carve any parts that you want to shape further. Sand any surfaces that look rough or uneven, and apply paint or finish.

SCROLL SAW INLAY

Although marquetry and intarsia projects look to be inlaid, they are not — the parts simply fit together like the pieces of a puzzle. However, you can use a scroll saw to inlay one piece of wood in another by using a combination of intarsia and bevel-cutting techniques.

You could simply stack the inlay stock on top of the background board, cut the inlay pattern in both pieces, and drop the sawed inlay into place in its background. However, because the saw blade leaves a kerf, the inlay will not fit as well as it might if you cut both boards on a slight bevel. So, tilt the worktable slightly and cut the perimeter of the inlay in *one direction* only, making the inlay just a little bigger than the piece you're removing from the background. When the inlay drops into place, it will fit perfectly with no visible kerf around the edges.

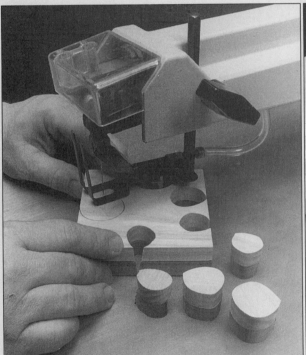 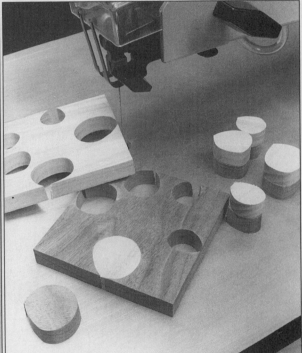

1   **The trick is to find the right** bevel angle. It will be different for every project, depending on the thickness of the stock and the size of the blade, and you must make a few test cuts to find it. Stack two scraps face to face, tilt the table to the left a few degrees, and cut a circle clockwise in the scraps. Fit the circular piece from the top scrap into the hole in the bottom scrap. If the circle drops below the surface, increase the tilt. If it won't drop down flush with the surface, decrease the tilt.

(continued) ▷

SCROLL SAW INLAY — CONTINUED

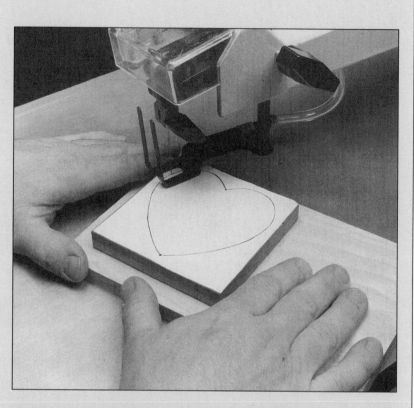

2 **Once you've found the** proper bevel angle, stack the inlay stock on top of the background board. Fasten the two pieces together with carpet tape to keep them from shifting. Cut the shape of the inlay, sawing clockwise around the perimeter. Separate the pieces and discard the tape.

3 **Test fit the inlay in the recess** you've sawed in the background. You may have a little work to do with a file to get it to fit perfectly. When it fits to your satisfaction, glue it in place. Let the glue dry overnight, then sand the surface to make the inlay and the background perfectly flush.

SCROLL SAW JOINERY

Although most craftsmen don't think of the scroll saw as a joinery tool, it can be used to make several common woodworking joints.

COPED JOINTS

To make a coped joint, mate two shaped boards, cutting one board to the exact reverse or *negative* shape of the other. Butt the two shapes — the positive and the negative — together. Coped joints are used primarily in finish carpentry to join moldings and sashwork. The end of a molding is cut to the negative shape of the adjoining molding, then butted against it.

Traditionally, coped joints are made with a coping saw, but you can also use a scroll saw to cut the negative shapes, provided the molding lies *flat*. (This technique won't work for crown moldings, which are

installed at an angle.) Cut the first piece of molding to length, cutting the adjoining end square. Measure the length of the second piece and *miter* the adjoining end. (SEE FIGURE 5-21.) Using a scroll saw, cut along the arris where the mitered surface meets the shaped surface. This will create the negative shape. (SEE FIGURE 5-22.) Fit the coped end of the second molding to the shaped surface of the first. (SEE FIGURE 5-23.)

TRY THIS TRICK

If you're cutting long pieces of molding and find it difficult to turn them on the scroll saw, use a spiral blade. Because spiral blades cut in all directions, you don't have to turn the work at all.

5-21 When joining two pieces of molding square to one another with a coped joint, you butt the end of one molding against the shaped surface of the other. To do this, you must saw the end to a precise *negative* of the molded shape. Miter the adjoining end at 45 degrees, and darken the arris where the mitered surface meets the shaped surface with a pencil. The arris line is where you want to cut.

5-22 Cut along the darkened arris line. Some craftsmen prefer to undercut coped joints slightly for a better fit. To undercut, tilt the table 5 to 10 degrees. Mount a spiral blade in the scroll saw and rest the molding on the lower side of the table, parallel to the direction of the table tilt. (It should stick out to the side.) Cut along the arris *without* turning the molding.

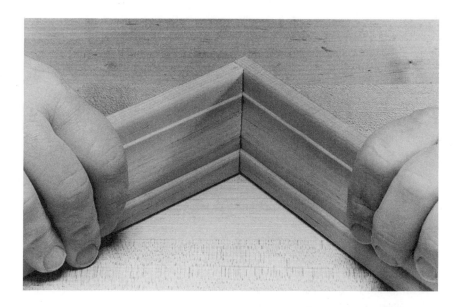

5-23 Butt the coped end of the molding against the shaped surface of the other. If there are any gaps in the joint, adjust the negative shape on the coped end with a file or a bench knife.

SLIP JOINTS AND BRIDLE JOINTS

To make a slip joint, cut a deep notch in the edge of each adjoining piece, then slip the notched edges together. To make a bridle joint, cut a deep notch in the end of one piece and a tenon in the end of the other. Slip the notch over the tenon. You can use a scroll saw to cut the notches in both joints. (SEE FIGURE 5-24.)

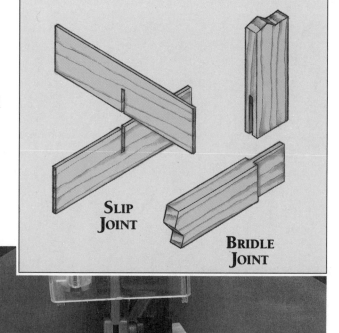

SLIP JOINT

BRIDLE JOINT

5-24 Use a scroll saw to cut the deep notches and long tenons needed to make slip joints and bridle joints. Use a large scroll (jigsaw) blade when cutting the long, straight sides of each notch or tenon. The cuts will seem to take forever if you use a smaller fret (scroll saw) blade. Even so, take your time — if you rush the cut, the blade may wander and the sides will be bowed or wavy. After sawing the sides of a notch, cut across the bottom and remove the waste. If necessary, use the blade to nibble away the stock at the bottom of the notch.

MITER JOINTS

You can use a scroll saw to true up a poorly fitting miter joint. Put the mitered ends together so the boards are precisely 90 degrees to one another, then cut along the joint with a fine blade. The blade will shave each end so it fits perfectly with the other. (SEE FIGURE 5-25.)

You can also cut corner joints on a scroll saw, using some intarsia procedures. You don't have to make straight cuts at 45 degrees for the corners to fit. In fact, you can cut decorative joints that fit more like coped joints than miters. (SEE FIGURE 5-26.)

5-25 To true up a poorly fitting miter joint on a scroll saw, first cut a scrap of plywood or particleboard with a perfectly square corner. Hold the adjoining boards against the edges of this scrap so they are 90 degrees from one another, and press the mitered ends together. Saw along the miter joint with a fine scroll saw blade. Even if you don't cut perfectly straight, the blade will shave the ends of both boards so they fit perfectly. Depending on how badly the miter joint fits when you begin, you may have to repeat this process several times to true the joint.

5-26 To cut miters or decorative corner joints on a scroll saw, lap the ends of the boards that you want to join. Fasten the boards face to face with carpet tape: The boards should be square to one another, and the end of each board should be flush with the outside edge of the other. Lay out the corner joint on the top board in the stack, then cut through both boards at once. Remove the scraps and the tape and fit the corner joint together. No matter what design you saw, the joint should fit perfectly.

DOVETAILS

You can use a scroll saw instead of a dovetail saw when making dovetail joints. Make the pins first — cut the cheeks with the worktable tilted, then cut along the baseline with a chisel to free the waste. (SEE FIGURES 5-27 AND 5-28.) Use the completed pins to mark the tails. Readjust the worktable square to the blade, and cut both the cheeks and the baseline with the scroll saw. (SEE FIGURE 5-29.)

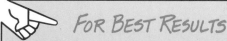

FOR BEST RESULTS

With the exception of slip joints and bridle joints, most joinery can be cut using precision-ground blades in the scroll saw. They cut slightly faster and smoother, but the real advantage is that they give you more control, allowing greater precision.

5-27 When using a scroll saw to make dovetails, cut the pins first. Tilt the table to the left approximately 10 degrees and saw one side or *cheek* on each pin. Then tilt the table the same number of degrees to the right and cut the remaining cheeks. **Note:** The worktable of your scroll saw must tilt both right and left to do this. You can't make an auxiliary tilting table as you would if performing this operation on a band saw. With only a 2-inch thickness capacity, there's no room to mount the table.

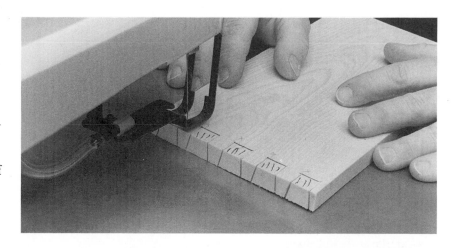

5-28 Remove the waste between the pins with a chisel. Place the edge of the chisel on the baseline and give it a sharp blow with a mallet to cut down about 1/16 inch. Then use the chisel as a wedge to lift a 1/16-inch-thick chip out from between the pins. Repeat until all the waste is removed.

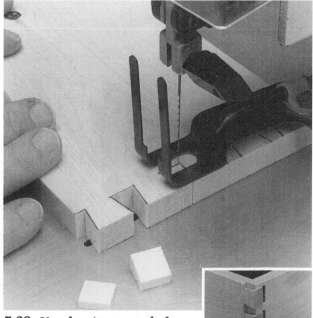

5-29 Use the pins to mark the tails on the adjoining board. Readjust the worktable square to the blade. Saw the cheeks *and* the baseline to remove the waste — there's no need to use the chisel for this step in the procedure.

PROJECTS

6

SHOP-MADE SCROLL SAW

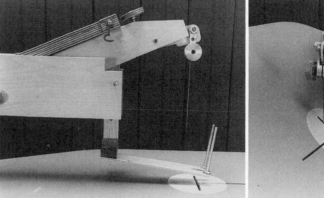

$\mathbf{A}$re you new to scroll work and looking for an inexpensive machine to try out? Do you have only an occasional need for a scroll saw and can't justify purchasing an expensive machine? Are you on a budget and need a better machine than you can afford to buy? Or do you like the satisfaction of working with tools you have made? If you can answer yes to any of these questions, consider building a scroll saw.

You can build the benchtop scroll saw shown for about the price of a small, no-frills commercial machine, and the homemade model will do so much more. Here are some of its features:

- Big 20-inch throat capacity and 2-inch thickness capacity
- Quick-release blade clamps and up-front tension adjustment for quick blade changes
- Lifting top arm to help thread blades through holes for interior cuts
- Table that tilts 45 degrees right *and* left
- Sand-filled base to reduce vibration
- Built-in blade storage

To simplify construction, the machine is powered by a saber saw mounted in the base. You can use almost any saber saw. If you mount a variable-speed saw, you'll be able to change the speeds of the scroll saw. If you use a single-speed saw, plug it into a router speed controller to vary the speeds.

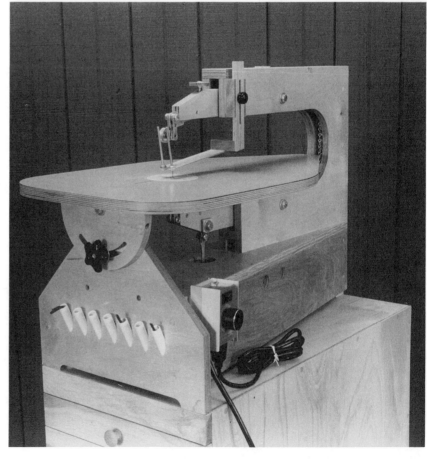

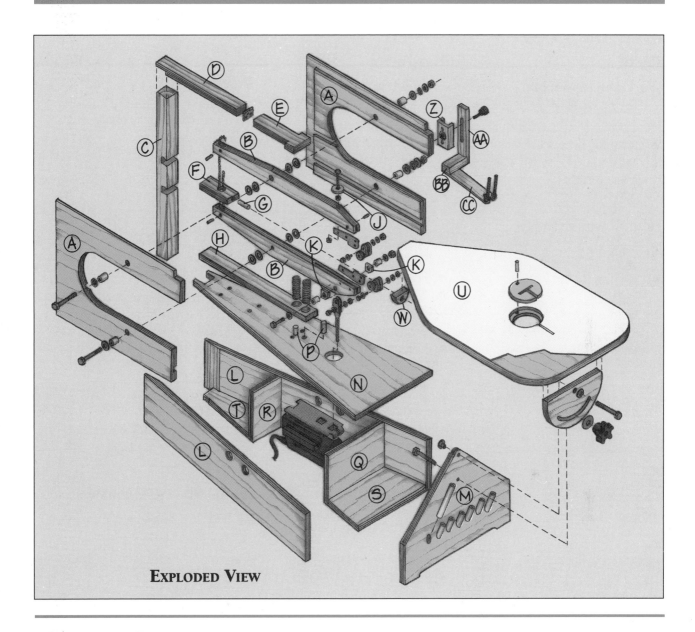

EXPLODED VIEW

MATERIALS LIST (FINISHED DIMENSIONS)

Parts

Frame/Arm Assembly

A. Right/left
   frame (2) $^{3}/_{4}$" x 14" x 18$^{1}/_{2}$"
B. Arms (2) $^{3}/_{4}$" x 2" x 21"
C. Post*   1$^{1}/_{2}$" x 1$^{3}/_{4}$" x 20$^{1}/_{2}$"†
D. Fixed frame
   top $^{3}/_{4}$" x 1$^{3}/_{4}$" x 12"
E. Lifting frame
   top $^{3}/_{4}$" x 2$^{1}/_{2}$" x 6$^{1}/_{2}$"
F. Pivot mount $^{3}/_{4}$" x 1$^{3}/_{4}$" x 4$^{1}/_{4}$"
G. Pivot $^{3}/_{8}$" dia. x 2"

H. Rib $^{3}/_{4}$" x 1$^{3}/_{4}$" x 16"
J. Tension knob   1$^{1}/_{2}$" dia. x $^{1}/_{4}$"
K. Spacers (2) $^{1}/_{4}$" x 1" x 1"

Base Assembly

L. Sides (2) $^{3}/_{4}$" x 6"† x 29$^{11}/_{16}$"
M. Front $^{3}/_{4}$" x 12$^{13}/_{16}$"† x 16"
N. Base top $^{3}/_{4}$" x 11$^{3}/_{4}$" x 29$^{1}/_{4}$"
P. Spring locator
   dowels (2) $^{5}/_{8}$" dia. x 1$^{1}/_{2}$"

Q. Front divider $^{3}/_{4}$" x 6"† x 8$^{1}/_{8}$"
R. Back divider $^{3}/_{4}$" x 6"† x 4$^{1}/_{8}$"
S. Front
   bottom $^{3}/_{4}$" x 6$^{3}/_{4}$" x 10$^{1}/_{4}$"
T. Back bottom $^{3}/_{4}$" x 3$^{7}/_{8}$" x 7$^{3}/_{4}$"

*Make this part from solid wood.

†These dimensions may change depending on the saber saw used to power the
scroll saw.   (continued) ▷

MATERIALS LIST — CONTINUED

Parts

Worktable Assembly

U.	Worktable	3/4″ x 16″ x 28″
V.	Trunnion	3/4″ x 4½″ x 8″
W.	Pivot block	3/4″ x 1¼″ x 2″
X.	Table insert	3¾″ dia. x ¼″
Y.	Insert locator dowel	3/16″ dia. x ½″

Hold-Down Assembly

Z.	Hold-down guide*	3/4″ x 1½″ x 2¾″
AA.	Hold-down leg*	3/8″ x 1″ x 6½″
BB.	Hold-down ankle*	3/4″ x 1″ x 2½″
CC.	Hold-down foot	1/8″ x 1⅜″ x 7⅛″

*Make these parts from solid wood.

†These dimensions may change depending on the saber saw used to power the scroll saw.

Hardware

Frame/Arm Assembly

#8 x 1¼″ Flathead wood screws (16)
3/8″ x 3″ Hex bolts (2)
3/8″ x 2¼″ Hex bolt
1/4″ x 1¼″ Hex bolts (3)
#10 x 2″ Carriage bolt
#8 x 1″ Flathead machine screws (2)
5/16″ Flat washers (8)
3/16″ Flat washers (10–14)
#10 Flat washer
#8 Flat washers (2)
3/8″ Stop nuts (3)
1/4″ Stop nuts (3)
#10 Hex nuts (2)
#8 Hex nuts (2)
3/8″ I.D. x 1/32″ thk. Spring washers (2)
3/8″ I.D. x 9/16″ O.D. x 3/8″ lg. Nylon bushing (10)
3/8″ I.D. x 1/16″ thk. Nylon flat washers (8)
1/4″ x 3/4″ lg. Spring pins (3)
.082″ x 7/8″ dia. x 2½″ lg. Compression springs (2)
1½″ x 1½″ Hinge and mounting screws
1¼″ Hook and eye
#16 Single steel jack chain (24″)
1/8″ x 1¼″ x 1¼″ Aluminum angle (12″)

1/16″ x 3/4″ Steel bar (12″)
Quick-release blade clamps for 24″ Excalibur scroll saw (2)

Base Assembly

#8 x 1¼″ Flathead wood screws (26)
3/8″ T-nut
1/2″ I.D. PVC pipe (36″)
Saber saw

Worktable Assembly

#8 x 1¾″ Flathead wood screws (2)
#8 x 1½″ Flathead wood screws (2)
3/8″ x 2½″ Hex bolts (2)
3/8″ Fender washer
5/16″ Flat washer
3/8″ Star knob
100-grit Self-stick sandpaper
16″ x 28″ Heavy-duty plastic laminate

Hold-Down Assembly

#8 x 1″ Flathead wood screws (2)
#10 x 3″ Carriage bolts (2)
#10 Flat washers (3)
#10 Hex nuts (2)
#10 T-nut
3/4″ dia. Knob with #10 x 5/8″ lg. stud

PLAN OF PROCEDURE

1 Select the stock and cut the parts to size.
To make this project, you need 1 board foot of 4/4 (four-quarters) hardwood lumber, a 2-inch hardwood turning square 24 inches long, a sheet of 3/4-inch Baltic birch or Apple-ply plywood, a scrap of 1/4-inch plywood, and a scrap of 1/8-inch plywood. Use the hardest wood available for the solid wood parts. The scroll saw shown is made from Baltic birch plywood and rock maple.

When shopping for the hardware, there are several special considerations:

■ Look for *grade 5* hex bolts — these are harder and more precisely made. A grade 5 bolt has three lines cast into the head.

■ Many of the flat washers specified here are one size smaller than their bolts. This is not a mistake; the washers will still fit the bolts, but you'll get a closer fit.

■ Several of the hex bolts that are used as pivots are longer than needed and must be cut to length. That's because bolts of the proper length have a threaded portion which would be too long, and the threads may eat up the bushings or enlarge the pivot holes as the

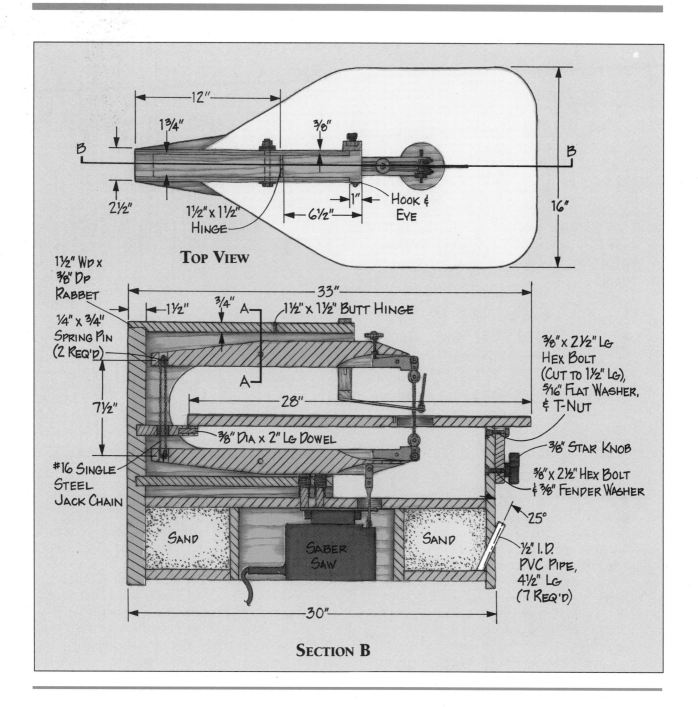

TOP VIEW

12"

1¾"

⅜"

2½"

1½" x 1½"
Hinge

6½"

1"

HOOK &
EYE

16"

SECTION B

1½" WD x
⅜" DP
RABBET

¼" x ¾"
SPRING PIN
(2 REQ'D)

1½"

¾"

A

1½" x 1½" BUTT HINGE

33"

⅜" x 2½" LG
HEX BOLT
(CUT TO 1½" LG),
⁵⁄₁₆" FLAT WASHER,
& T-NUT

7½"

A

28"

⅜" DIA x 2" LG DOWEL

⅜" STAR KNOB

#16 SINGLE
STEEL
JACK CHAIN

⅜" x 2½" HEX BOLT
& ⅜" FENDER WASHER

25°

SAND

SABER
SAW

SAND

½" I.D.
PVC PIPE,
4½" LG
(7 REQ'D)

30"

machine runs. For this reason, you must buy bolts with an *unthreaded* shaft of the right length, then cut off the excess threads.

You can purchase most of the hardware listed at a good hardware store, with the exception of the quick-release blade clamps.

WHERE TO FIND IT

Order the quick-release blade clamps from:

Seyco
1414 Cranford Drive
Garland, TX 75047

Be sure to ask for the clamps made for the *24-inch* Excalibur scroll saw.

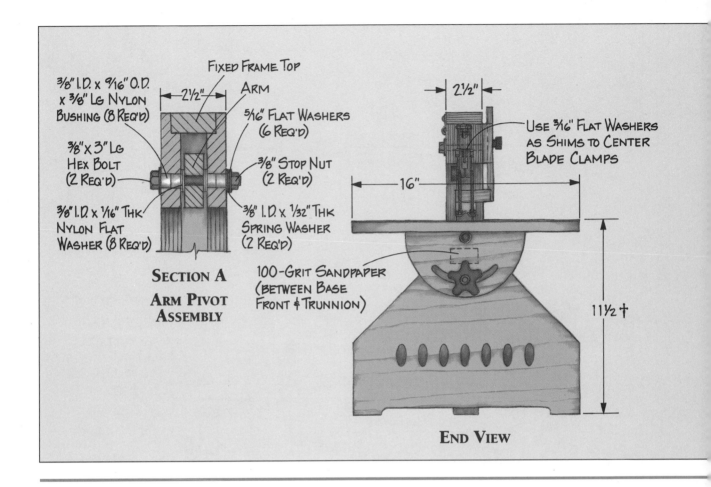

FIXED FRAME TOP

ARM

⅜" I.D. x 9/16" O.D. x ⅜" LG NYLON BUSHING (8 REQ'D)

2½"

5/16" FLAT WASHERS (6 REQ'D)

⅜" x 3" LG HEX BOLT (2 REQ'D)

⅜" STOP NUT (2 REQ'D)

⅜" I.D. x 1/16" THK NYLON FLAT WASHER (8 REQ'D)

⅜" I.D. x 1/32" THK SPRING WASHER (2 REQ'D)

SECTION A
ARM PIVOT
ASSEMBLY

100-GRIT SANDPAPER (BETWEEN BASE FRONT & TRUNNION)

2½"

USE 3/16" FLAT WASHERS AS SHIMS TO CENTER BLADE CLAMPS

16"

11½ †

END VIEW

Once you have gathered all the wood and hardware, measure the height and length of the saber saw you will use to drive the scroll saw. If the saber saw is longer than 11 inches, you may have to move the back divider in the base closer to the post. If it's taller than 6 inches, you'll have to increase the width of the base sides and divider and increase the height of the post and base front. The dimensions that will be affected are marked with a † on the Materials List and the working drawings.

Cut the parts to the sizes needed *except* for the front and back bottoms. Wait until after you've assembled most of the base parts to make these.

2   Make the frame.   As shown in the *Right Frame Layout,* the frames are joined to the post, frame top, rib, and pivot mount with rabbets and grooves. These joints are all drawn ⅜ inch deep. However, the actual depth will depend on the thickness of the plywood you're using to make the frame and the arms. Even though you've purchased ¾-inch plywood, you'll find it's slightly thinner than ¾ inch. You must

adjust the depth of the rabbets and grooves to compensate — if you don't, there will be too much slop when you assemble the arm pivots and the arms will slide from side to side while the machine is running.

To find the true depth of the frame joinery, cut three small scraps, about 2 inches square, from the same plywood you used to make the frame and arms. Drill a ⅜-inch-diameter hole in one piece and 9/16-inch-diameter holes in the other two. File four of the ⅜-inch-long nylon bushings 1/32 to 1/16 inch shorter than the others. (Mark these short bushings so you can easily identify them later.) Assemble the scraps along with the hardware shown in *Section A* as if you were making a pivot. *Use one long and one short bushing on each side;* otherwise, the bushings will protrude, since the plywood is thinner than ¾ inch.

Measure the thickness of the assembly, from the outside surface of one scrap to the outside surface of the other. It will probably be slightly less than the 2½ inches shown in *Section A.* Subtract the actual thickness from 2½, divide the result by 2, and make the joinery that much deeper. For example, if the

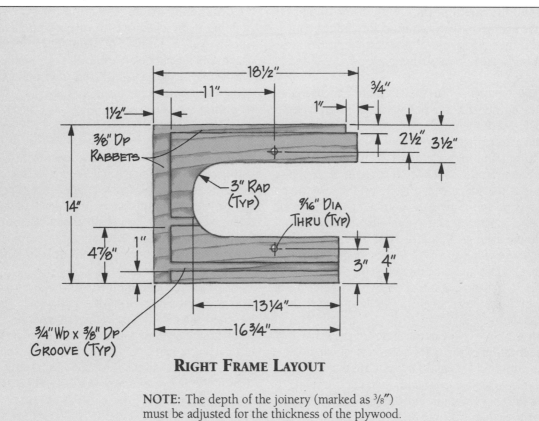

RIGHT FRAME LAYOUT

NOTE: The depth of the joinery (marked as $^3/_8''$) must be adjusted for the thickness of the plywood.

thickness measures $2^7/_{16}$ inches, make the joinery $^1/_{32}$ inch deeper — $(2^1/_2 - 2^7/_{16}) \div 2 = ^1/_{32}$. Cut the rabbets and grooves $^{13}/_{32}$ inch deep — $^3/_8 + ^1/_{32} = ^{13}/_{32}$.

Stack the right and left frames face to face so the ends and edges are flush. Hold the stack together with double-faced carpet tape. Lay out the profile of the frame, along with the rabbets, grooves, and holes. Cut the joinery in the exposed faces on a table-mounted router or a dado cutter. (*SEE FIGURE 6-1.*) Drill $^9/_{16}$-inch-diameter holes for the arm pivots, then saw the profile with a band saw or saber saw. Sand the sawed edges.

6-1 Cut the joinery in the right and left frames with the parts stacked face to face. (The edges and ends must be perfectly flush.) Set up to make a rabbet or a groove, cut one exposed face, then turn the stack over and cut the other. Repeat until you have cut all the joints. Keep the stack together when drilling the pivot holes and cutting the frame profile. When you take the stack apart, the surfaces you cut will become the inside faces. The right and left frames should be mirror images of each other.

3 **Make the metal parts.** With the exception of the blade clamps, which you must buy from a commercial source, all the metal parts can be made from aluminum or steel stock with a hacksaw, a file, and a drill press.

■ *Blade mounts* — Cut the aluminum angle stock along the corner to make two pieces of ⅛-inch-thick bar stock. Stack the pieces face to face, holding them together with carpet tape. Lay out the profile of the blade mount and the location of the mounting holes for the blade clamps, as shown in the *Basic Blade Mount Layout.* Cut the shape with a hacksaw, then clean up the edges and round over the corners with a file. Drill the ³/₁₆-inch-diameter and ¼-inch-diameter holes.

■ *Pitman arms* — From the steel bar stock, cut two pieces ⅝ inch wide and 1¹¹/₁₆ inches long. Stack the parts face to face and tape them together. Mark and drill the ⅜-inch-diameter and ¼-inch-diameter holes, as shown in the *Pitman Arm Layout.* Round over the top ends with a file.

■ *Drive link* — Lay out the shape of the drive link and the location of the pivot hole on steel bar stock, as shown in the *Drive Link Layout.* Drill the ¼-inch-diameter hole near the top end, then cut the shape and file the edges smooth. If necessary, use a file to chamfer the edges near the bottom end, as shown in *Section C,* so the drive link fits in the blade chuck on your saber saw.

FOR BEST RESULTS

Polish the flat faces of the pitman arms and drive link where the metal parts will rub together.

4 **Make the arms.** Stack the arms face to face, holding them together with carpet tape. Mark the profile and the location of the holes as shown in the *Basic Arm Layout/Side View.* Drill the ⅜-inch-diameter pivot holes and the ¼-inch-diameter holes for the pins that will lock the chain in place. Cut the profile and sand the sawed edges. Then take the stack apart and discard the tape.

Rout or drill the ⁵/₁₆-inch-wide, ¹⁵/₁₆-inch-long slots near the rear ends of the arms, as shown in the *Basic Arm Layout/Top View.* Drill a ½-inch-diameter counterbore in the lower edge of the upper arm, near the front end, as shown in the *Upper Arm Modification/Side View.* Then drill a ³/₁₆-inch-diameter hole through the counterbore. Cut the ⅛-inch-wide slot for the blade mount with a table saw, but don't drill the blade mount pivot hole yet. (*SEE FIGURE 6-2.*)

Also cut a blade mount slot in the lower arm, as shown in the *Lower Arm Modification/Side View.* Drill ⁹/₁₆-inch-diameter holes in the arm and the spacers for the pitman arm pivot, then cut the slot for the pitman arm. The pitman slot is ⁵/₁₆ inch wide, as shown in the *Lower Arm Modification/End View.* Don't drill the holes that hold the blade mount in place yet.

5 **Install the blade mounts in the arms.** Cut and drill the tension knob for the upper arm, as shown in the *Blade Tension Assembly.* Mount a #10 hex nut on the end of a long carriage bolt, then force the nut into the ½-inch-diameter counterbore in the bottom edge of the arm. Remove the carriage bolt, but leave the nut in the counterbore. Secure a #10 x 2-inch carriage bolt through the center of the tension knob with a hex nut.

6-2 The front ends of the arms must be slotted to hold the blade mounts. The lower arm requires an additional slot for the pitman arms. You can make all these slots with a table saw and an ordinary combination blade. Use the fence to guide the arm and a stop to halt the cut when the slot is the proper length.

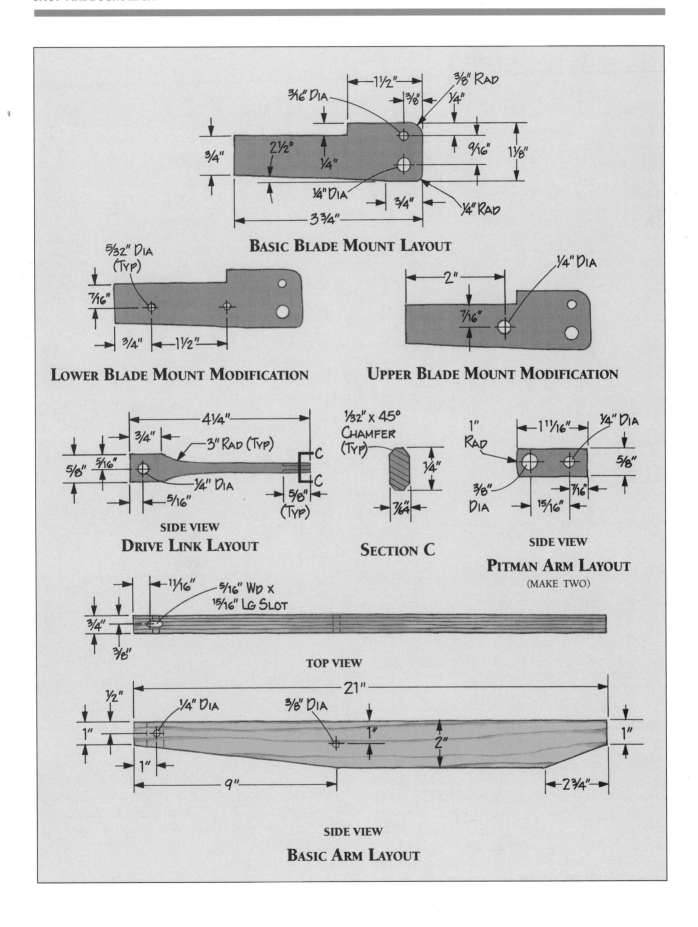

BASIC BLADE MOUNT LAYOUT

LOWER BLADE MOUNT MODIFICATION

UPPER BLADE MOUNT MODIFICATION

SIDE VIEW
DRIVE LINK LAYOUT

SECTION C

SIDE VIEW
PITMAN ARM LAYOUT
(MAKE TWO)

TOP VIEW

SIDE VIEW
BASIC ARM LAYOUT

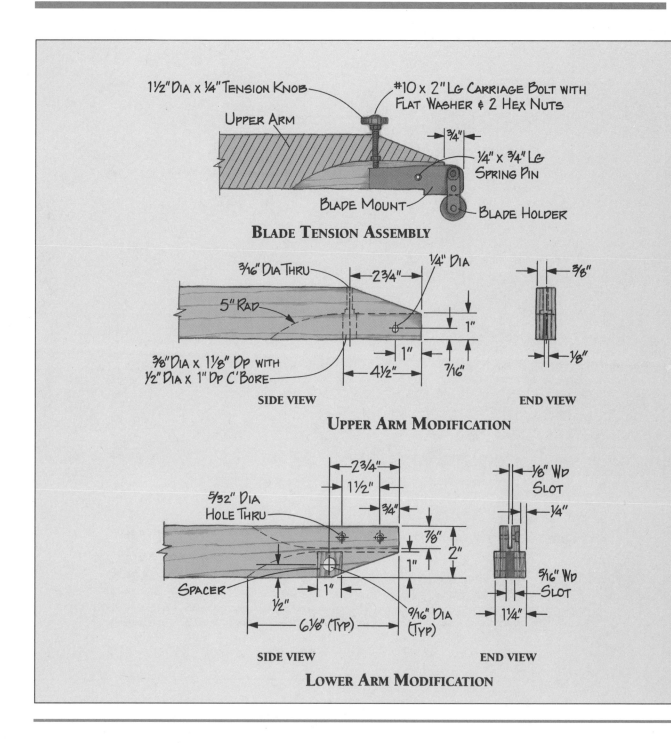

BLADE TENSION ASSEMBLY

UPPER ARM MODIFICATION

LOWER ARM MODIFICATION

Slide the upper blade mount into its slot. The lower edge of the blade mount should be flush with the lower edge of the arm, and the mount should protrude 3/4 inch from the end of the arm. Squeeze the arm with a clamp so the blade mount won't move, and drill the 1/4-inch-diameter pivot hole. You must be very careful to keep the bit clear of chips as you drill, or the hole will be oversize. Drill a little, retract the bit and blow away the chips, drill a little more, and repeat until you have drilled through both the arm and the blade mount. Drive a 1/4-inch-diameter spring pin in the pivot hole, and install the tension knob assembly in the 3/16-inch-diameter hole in the top of the arm, threading it through the nut that you pressed into the counterbore.

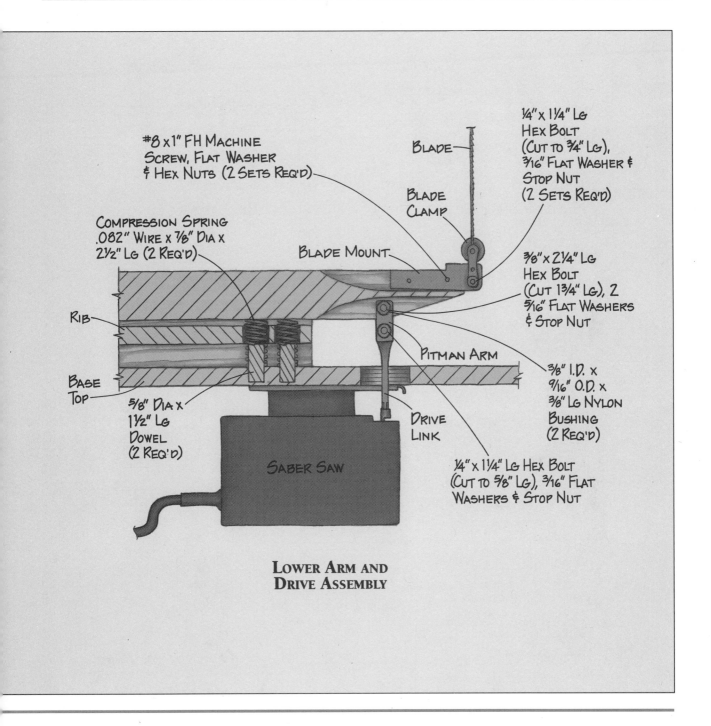

#8 x 1" FH MACHINE SCREW, FLAT WASHER & HEX NUTS (2 SETS REQ'D)

COMPRESSION SPRING .082" WIRE x ⅞" DIA x 2½" LG (2 REQ'D)

BLADE MOUNT

RIB

BASE TOP

⅝" DIA x 1½" LG DOWEL (2 REQ'D)

SABER SAW

BLADE

BLADE CLAMP

PITMAN ARM

DRIVE LINK

¼" x 1¼" LG HEX BOLT (CUT TO ¾" LG), ³⁄₁₆" FLAT WASHER & STOP NUT (2 SETS REQ'D)

⅜" x 2¼" LG HEX BOLT (CUT 1¾" LG), 2 ⁵⁄₁₆" FLAT WASHERS & STOP NUT

⅜" I.D. x ⁹⁄₁₆" O.D. x ⅜" LG NYLON BUSHING (2 REQ'D)

¼" x 1¼" LG HEX BOLT (CUT TO ⅝" LG), ³⁄₁₆" FLAT WASHERS & STOP NUT

LOWER ARM AND DRIVE ASSEMBLY

To attach the lower blade mount, position it in the lower arm exactly as the upper mount is positioned in the upper arm. Secure it with a clamp, and drill two ⁵⁄₃₂-inch-diameter holes through the arm and the clamp. Countersink the holes, remove the clamp, and fasten the blade mount in the arm with #8 machine screws, washers, and nuts, as shown in the *Lower Arm and Drive Assembly.*

Glue the spacers to the faces of the lower arm, as shown in the *Lower Arm Modification/Side View.* Use two of the nylon bushings to keep the ⁹⁄₁₆-inch-diameter holes in all the parts aligned while the glue dries. When it has dried, remove the bushings and sand the bottom edges of the spacers flush with the bottom edge of the arm.

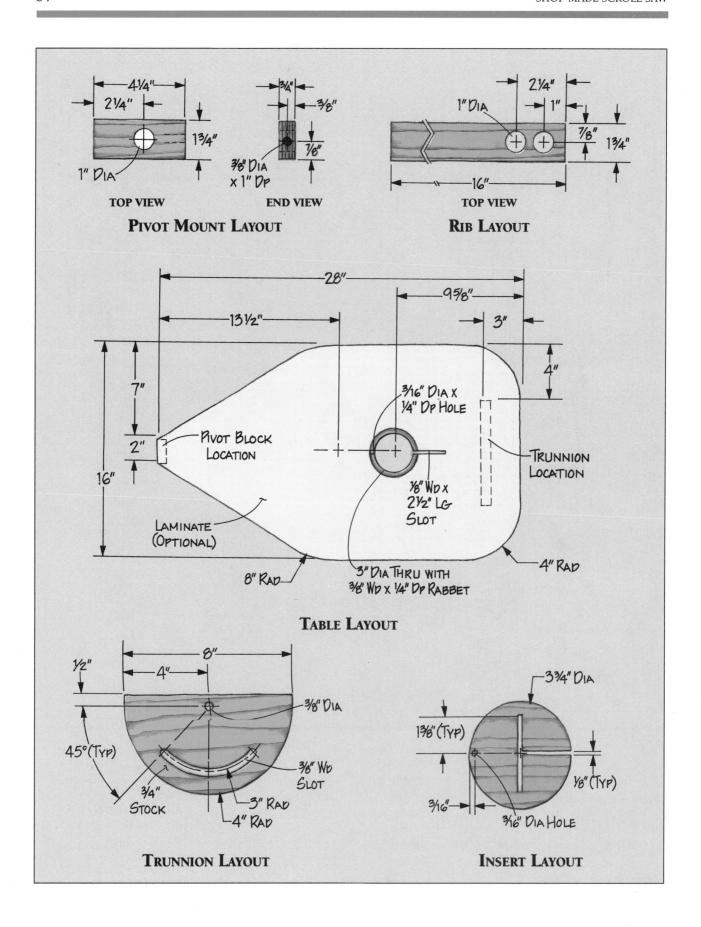

PIVOT MOUNT LAYOUT

4¼"
2¼"
3/8"
1¾"
1" DIA
TOP VIEW
3/8" DIA x 1" DP
7/8"
END VIEW

RIB LAYOUT

2¼"
1" DIA
1"
7/8"
1¾"
16"
TOP VIEW

TABLE LAYOUT

28"
9⅝"
13½"
3"
4"
7"
3/16" DIA x ¼" DP HOLE
2"
PIVOT BLOCK LOCATION
16"
⅛" WD x 2½" LG SLOT
TRUNNION LOCATION
LAMINATE (OPTIONAL)
8" RAD
3" DIA THRU WITH 3/8" WD x ¼" DP RABBET
4" RAD

TRUNNION LAYOUT

½"
8"
4"
3/8" DIA
45° (TYP)
3/8" WD SLOT
¾" STOCK
3" RAD
4" RAD

INSERT LAYOUT

3¾" DIA
1⅜" (TYP)
⅛" (TYP)
3/16"
3/16" DIA HOLE

6 **Make the post, frame top parts, pivot mount, and rib.** Several of the remaining parts of the frame/arm assembly also need machining:

■ *Post* — Cut ¾-inch-wide, ¾-inch-deep dadoes in the front face of the post, as shown in the *Base/Side View*. These dadoes hold the rib and the pivot mount.

■ *Fixed frame top* — Cut a 1½-inch-wide, ⅜-inch-deep rabbet in the bottom surface of the back end to fit over the post, as shown in *Section B*.

■ *Lifting frame top* — Lay out and cut the profile of the frame top, as shown in the *Top View* on page 77. The ears on the front end fit the notches in the top edge of the right and left frames.

■ *Pivot mount* — Drill a 1-inch-diameter hole through the face, and a ⅜-inch-diameter, 1-inch-deep hole in the front end, as shown in the *Pivot Mount Layout*.

■ *Rib* — Drill two 1-inch-diameter holes through the face, as shown in the *Rib Layout*.

7 **Make the worktable and insert.** Cover the table stock with plastic laminate, then lay out the profile of the table and the location of the blade hole, as shown in the *Table Layout*. Cut the shape with a band saw or saber saw and sand the sawed edges.

Using a hole saw, cut a 3-inch-diameter blade hole through the table. Rout a ⅜-inch-wide, ¼-inch-deep rabbet around the circumference of the hole to create a ledge for the insert. Cut out the insert with a 4-inch hole saw, and sand the circumference until it fits snugly in the rabbet. **Note:** You may want to make several inserts while you're at it, and set some aside as spares.

Lay out the slots on the insert and the table, as shown in the *Insert Layout* and *Table Layout*. Cut the slots with a saber saw or coping saw. Put the insert in the table and line up the front slot with the slot in the worktable. Drill a ³⁄₁₆-inch-diameter, ½-inch-deep hole through the insert and into the worktable, toward the back edge. Remove the insert and glue the insert locator dowel in the hole in the worktable. Let the glue dry, then replace the insert and sand the top of the dowel flush with the surface of the insert.

8 **Make the trunnion and pivot block.** Lay out the profile of the trunnion and the locations of the pivot hole and the curved slot, as shown in the *Trunnion Layout*. Also lay out the pivot block, as shown in the *Pivot Block Layout*. Cut both the trunnion and the pivot block and sand the sawed edges. Drill ⅜-inch-diameter pivot holes through both parts. Rout the curved slot in the trunnion on a table-mounted router. *(SEE FIGURE 6-3.)*

6-3 To rout the curved slot in the trunnion, first make the pivoting jig shown. Mount a ⅜-inch straight bit in a table-mounted router and clamp the jig to the table so the pivot and the bit are precisely 3 inches apart, as measured from the centers. Drill a ⅜-inch-diameter pivot hole *and a* starting hole where you've marked the slot, at one end. Adjust the router's depth of cut to rout about ⅛ inch deep. Place the trunnion on the pivot so the bit fits in the starter hole. Holding the stock down on the jig, turn the router on and swing the trunnion back and forth over the bit. Turn off the router, raise the bit another ⅛ inch, and cut again. Repeat until you have cut the slot through the trunnion.

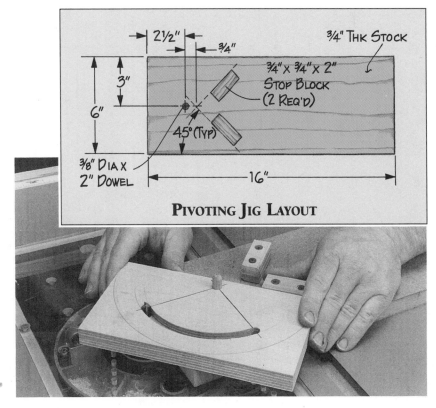

PIVOTING JIG LAYOUT

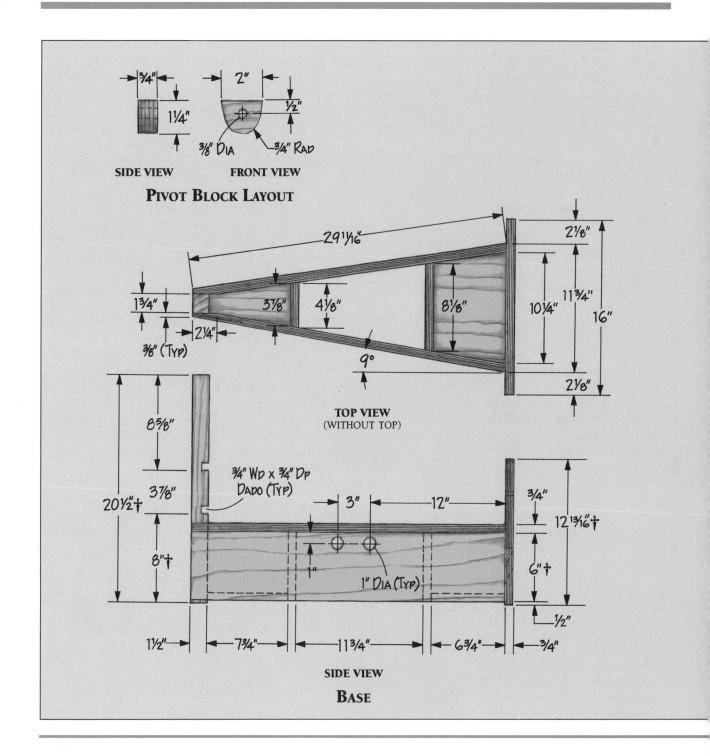

¾"
1¼"

2"
½"

⅜" Dɪᴀ   ¾" Rᴀᴅ

SIDE VIEW   FRONT VIEW

PIVOT BLOCK LAYOUT

29¹¹⁄₁₆"

2⅛"
11¾"
16"

1¾"
2¼"
⅜" (Tʏᴘ)

3⅞"   4⅛"

8⅛"

10¼"

9°

2⅛"

TOP VIEW
(WITHOUT TOP)

8⅝"

¾" Wᴅ x ¾" Dᴘ
Dᴀᴅᴏ (Tʏᴘ)

3"   12"

¾"
12¹³⁄₁₆"†

20½"†   3⅞"

1"

1" Dɪᴀ (Tʏᴘ)

6"†

½"

8"†

1½"   7¾"   11¾"   6¾"   ¾"

SIDE VIEW

BASE

9 **Make the base.** The tripod base is assembled with miter and butt joints. Miter the front ends of the sides and both ends of the dividers at 81 degrees, as shown in the *Base/Top View*. Miter the back ends of the sides at 9 degrees. (*SEE FIGURE 6-4.*)

Lay out the profile of the base front and the locations of the various holes, as shown in the *Base Front*

Layout/Front View. Counterbore and drill the ⁷⁄₁₆-inch-diameter pivot hole and the ⅜-inch-diameter hole for the table-tilt locking bolt. Also drill a line of ⅝-inch-diameter holes at 25 degrees through the front, as shown in the *Base Front Layout/Section D.* (*SEE FIGURE 6-5.*) These will hold the blade storage tubes.

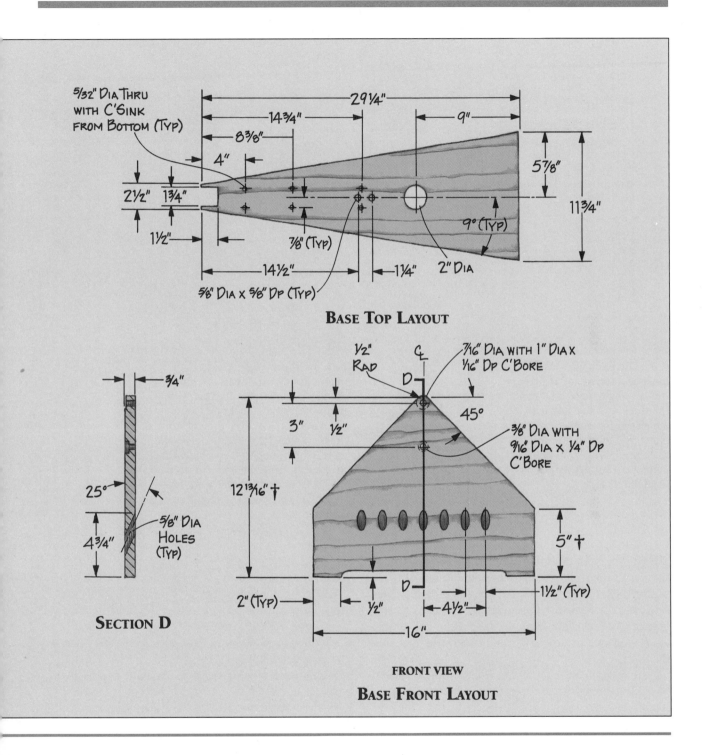

BASE TOP LAYOUT

SECTION D

FRONT VIEW
BASE FRONT LAYOUT

Lay out the profile of the base top and the location of the 2-inch-diameter drive link hole, the 5/8-inch-diameter holes that hold the spring locator dowels, and the 5/32-inch-diameter pilot holes for the screws that will hold the frame/arm assembly to the base assembly, as shown in the *Base Top Layout*. Cut the drive link hole with a hole saw, and drill the other holes. Also mark and drill the 1-inch-diameter ventilation holes in the sides, as shown in the *Base/Side View*.

When all the holes are drilled, cut the profiles of the base front and the base top. Sand the sawed edges. Assemble the sides, dividers, and front with glue and screws. Screw the post in place, but *don't* glue it to the sides.

6-4 The back ends of the sides must be mitered at 9 degrees, a smaller angle than you can cut with the stock laid face down on your table saw. To cut an extremely acute miter, you must hold the stock vertically. Secure the sides in a tenoning jig and use it to guide the wood past the angled blade.

6-5 Drill the angled ⁵⁄₈-inch- diameter holes in the base front for the blade storage tubes, using a brad-point bit. Tilt the drill press table so the work surface is 65 degrees from the bit, and secure a tall fence to the table to help support the work. Clamp the base front to the fence to keep the bit from pushing the work sideways. Feed the bit very slowly as you drill each hole.

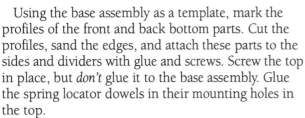

Using the base assembly as a template, mark the profiles of the front and back bottom parts. Cut the profiles, sand the edges, and attach these parts to the sides and dividers with glue and screws. Screw the top in place, but *don't* glue it to the base assembly. Glue the spring locator dowels in their mounting holes in the top.

Note: Countersink all screws. In addition, *counterbore* those screws that are used to reinforce glue joints, such as the screws that hold the base front to the sides. Cover the heads of the counterbored/countersunk screws with wooden plugs and sand the plugs flush with the surface.

10 Make the hold-down. All of the parts in the hold-down assembly need to be machined:

■ *Hold-down guide* — Cut a 1-inch-wide, ³⁄₈-inch-deep groove in the hold-down guide, as shown in the *Hold-Down Guide Layout/End View*. Then drill and counterbore a ¹⁄₄-inch-diameter hole for a T-nut, and

drill and countersink ⁵⁄₃₂-inch-diameter pilot holes for flathead wood screws.

■ *Hold-down leg* — Cut a ³⁄₄-inch-wide, ³⁄₁₆-inch-deep rabbet in the bottom end of the hold-down leg and rout a ³⁄₁₆-inch-wide slot through its face, as shown in the *Hold-Down Leg Layout/Top View*. Miter the bottom end at 7 degrees.

■ *Hold-down ankle* — Bevel the bottom face at 7 degrees, as shown in the *Hold-Down Ankle Layout*.

■ *Hold-down foot* — Lay out the profile and the location of the ³⁄₁₆-inch-diameter holes in the toes, as shown in the *Hold-Down Foot Layout*. Drill the holes, cut the profile, and sand the sawed edges.

Insert the #10 T-nut in the guide, and install #10 x 3-inch carriage bolts, washers, and nuts in the foot. (The long carriage bolts serve as blade guards.) Glue the ankle to the leg, but *don't* glue the foot to the ankle yet. Wait until after you've assembled the scroll saw and have mounted a blade.

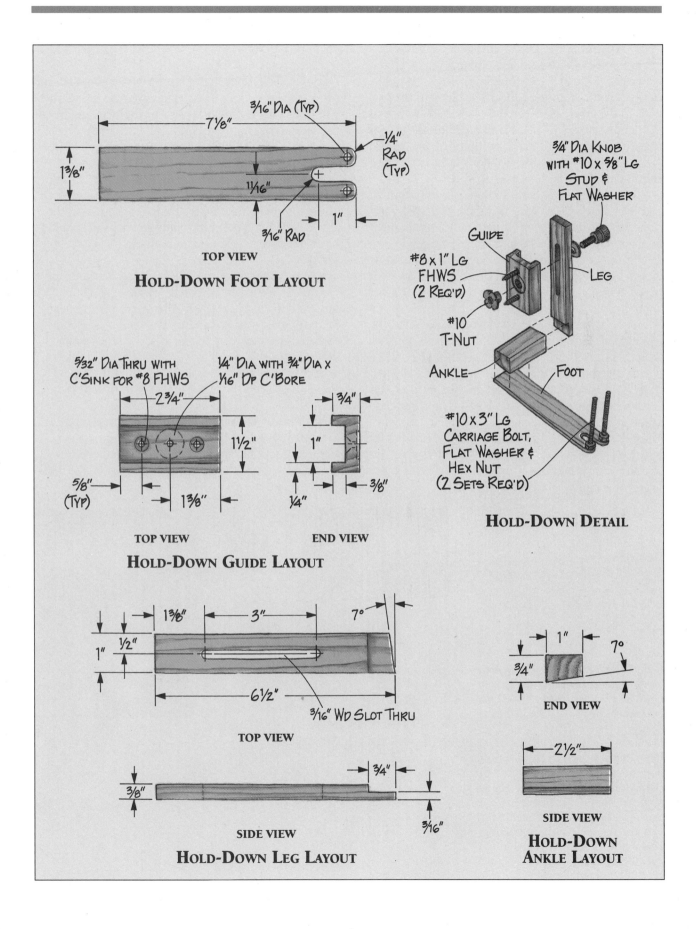

3/16" DIA (TYP)

7 1/8"

1/4" RAD (TYP)

1 3/8"

11/16"

3/16" RAD

1"

TOP VIEW

HOLD-DOWN FOOT LAYOUT

3/4" DIA KNOB WITH #10 x 5/8" LG STUD & FLAT WASHER

GUIDE

#8 x 1" LG FHWS (2 REQ'D)

LEG

#10 T-NUT

ANKLE

FOOT

#10 x 3" LG CARRIAGE BOLT, FLAT WASHER & HEX NUT (2 SETS REQ'D)

HOLD-DOWN DETAIL

5/32" DIA THRU WITH C'SINK FOR #8 FHWS

1/4" DIA WITH 3/4" DIA x 1/16" DP C'BORE

2 3/4"

3/4"

1 1/2"

1"

5/8" (TYP)

1 3/8"

1/4"

3/8"

TOP VIEW   **END VIEW**

HOLD-DOWN GUIDE LAYOUT

1 3/8"

3"

7°

1"

1/2"

6 1/2"

3/16" WD SLOT THRU

TOP VIEW

1"

7°

3/4"

END VIEW

3/8"

3/4"

3/16"

SIDE VIEW

HOLD-DOWN LEG LAYOUT

2 1/2"

SIDE VIEW

HOLD-DOWN ANKLE LAYOUT

11 **Assemble the frame and arms.** Make a chain loop about 16 inches in circumference. *(SEE FIGURE 6-6.)* Thread the chain loop through the hole in the pivot mount, then attach the chain to the back ends of the arms, as shown in *Section B*. However, use 1/4-inch-diameter, 3/4-inch-long *wooden dowels* instead of spring pins to hold the chain in the arms. This is just a temporary assembly; you don't want to use the spring pins until the final assembly.

Assemble the arms, pivot mount, rib, right frame, and left frame *without* glue, using the pivot bolts to hold these parts together. Remember to install one long and one short bushing on each side in each pivot as you assemble them. Put the flat washers and spring washers in place, then tighten the stop nuts until the pivots are snug, but not so tight that the spring washers are collapsed.

Slip the frame/arm assembly over the post. Put the fixed frame top in place, then clamp the parts together. Drill pilot holes and install screws. Since you will be gluing together the right and left frame, post, fixed frame top, and rib, countersink *and* counterbore the screws used to assemble these parts. (Later, you can cover these screw heads with plugs.) Note that you just countersink the screw that holds the pivot mount in the frame, and don't cover it. This will enable you to remove the pivot block along with the arms and

chain should these parts ever require repair or replacement.

Loosen the screws that hold the post and the base top to the base assembly, then remove the top (along with the frame assembly). Turn the top over and install the screws that hold the right and left frames to the base top. Replace the base top and the frame assembly on the base and tighten the screws.

Hinge the lifting frame top to the front end of the fixed frame top. Install a hook and eye to secure the lifting top when the saw is running, as shown in the *Top View*. When you need to lift the top arm, snap the hook out of the eye and raise both the frame top and the arm.

Attach the quick-release blade clamps to the blade mounts with 1/4-inch hex bolts, washers, and stop nuts, as shown in the *Lower Arm and Drive Assembly*. You may need a few additional 3/16-inch washers for each clamp to serve as shims, as shown in the *End View*. (The actual number will depend on the thickness of the washers.) Use these to center the blade clamps and keep them from shifting from side to side.

12 **Mount the worktable.** Attach the trunnion to the base front with 3/8-inch x 2 1/2-inch hex bolts, washers, and a star knob, as shown in *Section B*. Attach the pivot block to the back end of the worktable with

6-6 To make the chain loop, drill two 1/4-inch-diameter, 1/2-inch-deep holes in a 3/4-inch-thick scrap. These holes must be exactly 7 1/2 inches apart, on center. Insert 1/4-inch-diameter, 1-inch-long dowels in the holes. Stretch the #16 chain around both dowels to form a loop, pull the chain tight, and mark where you will join the chain links. Cut or pry open the links, discard any extra chain, and join the ends of the remaining chain. Stretch the completed loop over the dowels — it should fit with very little room to spare.

glue and screws, and glue the pivot dowel in the pivot mount.

Place the table on the trunnion and insert the pivot in the pivot block. Slide the table back as far as it will go. Install a blade in the blade clamps, tension it, and adjust the position of the arms so they are level — the outside edges of the arms should be flush with the edges of the frame. Place the insert in the worktable, square the table to the blade, and adjust the position of the worktable on the trunnion so the blade is perfectly centered in the insert. Mark the position of the trunnion on the underside of the table, then attach the trunnion to the table with glue and screws.

Note: Countersink the screws that hold the trunnion and the pivot block to the table.

13 Install the hold-down. Attach the guide to the right frame with glue and #8 x 1-inch wood screws, as shown in the *End View*. Secure the leg and ankle assembly in the guide using a small knob with a threaded stud. Position the foot on the worktable so the toes straddle the blade. Check that the carriage bolts serving as blade guards are far enough forward that the upper blade clamp won't hit them. When you're satisfied with the position of the foot, glue it to the underside of the ankle.

14 Glue the frame together. Release the blade tension and dismount the blade from the blade clamps. Loosen the table pivot bolt and the tilt lock knob, and remove the worktable assembly. Remove the hold-down assembly from the right frame. Loosen the arm pivot bolts and the screw that holds the pivot mount in place, and remove the arms and the pivot mount from the frame. Remove the lifting frame top, along with the hinge, hook, and eye. Finally, loosen the screws that hold the post and the base top to the base side. Remove the frame assembly and the base top from the base assembly.

Loosen the screws that hold the left frame to the frame assembly and the base top. Remove the left frame, spread glue on the adjoining surfaces of the post, rib, fixed frame top, and base top, then screw the left frame back in place. Repeat for the right frame. Plug the counterbored screw holes and sand the plugs flush with the wood surface.

15 Finish the scroll saw. Replace the base top and frame assembly on the base and secure it with

screws. Finish sand all the wood surfaces, making sure the joints are clean and well fitted. However, be careful not to sand through the thin plywood veneer.

Remove all the hardware *except* the blade mounts and the tension nut from the arms. Disassemble the tension knob and set the hardware aside. Also disassemble the hold-down, removing all its hardware. Finish sand all wood surfaces of the arms, tension knob, lifting frame top, hold-down assembly, worktable assembly, and insert.

Remove the frame assembly and base top from the base. Apply several coats of tung oil to all wooden surfaces, including the inside of the base. Let the finish dry completely, then rub it out with #0000 steel wool and wax. Thoroughly buff the wax.

16 Assemble the scroll saw. Thread the chain loop through the pivot mount and attach the chain to the back ends of the arms with spring pins. Attach the pitman arms to the lower arm with a 3/8-inch x 2 1/4-inch hex bolt (cut to 1 3/4 inches long), nylon bushings, washers, and stop nut, as shown in the *Lower Arm and Drive Assembly*.

Place the compression springs over the spring locator dowels. (These springs take up any slop in the drive mechanism, making the saw run more smoothly.) Mount the arms and pivot mount in the frame. Tighten the stop nuts on the arm pivot bolts until the spring washers just begin to collapse. Don't overtighten them; the arms must pivot freely. Replace the lifting frame top, along with its hinge, hook, and eye. Reassemble the tension knob and its carriage bolt, and install the knob in the upper arm. Also attach the blade clamps to the blade mounts. Again, don't overtighten the stop nuts; the clamps, too, must pivot freely.

Note: Put a drop of 10W oil on the hardware that secures the blade clamps to their mounts. However, *don't* lubricate the arm pivots or the pivot bolt that holds the pitman arms — oil or grease may cause the nylon bushings and washers to deteriorate.

Cut blade storage tubes from 1/2-inch PVC plumbing pipe, mitering the bottom ends at 25 degrees, as shown in *Section B*. Tap the tubes into the angled holes in the base front so the mitered ends rest flat on the front bottom. Line the front and back compartments in the base with plastic bags, then fill the bags with sand. This will help to reduce the vibration of the running machine. If you ever need to remove the sand, simply lift the bags out of their compartments. Fasten the base top and frame/arm assembly to the base assembly with screws.

Turn the scroll saw over on its side. Install the drive link in the saber saw and attach the saber saw to the underside of the base top. *(SEE FIGURE 6-7.)* Attach the drive link to the pitman arms, being careful not to overtighten the stop nut. **Note:** Lubricate the drive link pivot bolt with lithium grease.

Push down the lower arm and drive assembly so the saw is at the bottom of its stroke. The top edge of the lower arm should be parallel to the horizontal edge of the frame. If it's not, adjust the vertical position of the drive link in the saber saw. If the lower arm is too high and there is no room to adjust it downward, cut a little from the length of the drive link. If the arm is too low and the link is too short to adjust it upwards, you may have to make a longer link.

Turn the scroll saw right-side up. Cut a 2-inch-wide, 3-inch-long square of 100-grit self-stick sandpaper and adhere it to the base front, just below the table pivot hole, as shown in the *End View* on page 78. Then install the worktable assembly with the pivot and locking bolts. Again, don't overtighten the pivot bolt; the table must pivot freely when the locking knob is loose.

Secure the hold-down assembly to the guide with the locking knob. Finally, mount a blade in the blade clamps, tension it, and install the table insert. And that's it — you're ready to saw!

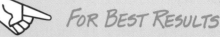

FOR BEST RESULTS

Lubricate the blade clamp pivots and drive link pivot every ten hours of operation, or every six months, whichever comes first. When not using the scroll saw, release the blade tension. Wood *creeps* under tension — that is, it becomes permanently deformed. If the blade remains tensioned all the time, the arms will eventually become bowed.

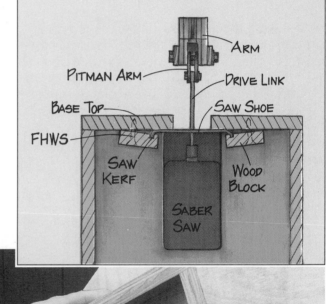

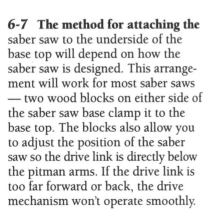

6-7 The method for attaching the saber saw to the underside of the base top will depend on how the saber saw is designed. This arrangement will work for most saber saws — two wood blocks on either side of the saber saw base clamp it to the base top. The blocks also allow you to adjust the position of the saber saw so the drive link is directly below the pitman arms. If the drive link is too far forward or back, the drive mechanism won't operate smoothly.

7

Scroll Saw
Storage Stand

If you're a serious scroller, you probably have dozens of scrolling tools in addition to your scroll saw. This sturdy stand makes use of the wasted space underneath your machine to store these items. There are six long, shallow drawers for patterns, manuals, spare blades, and other small tools, and one deeper drawer for larger scrolling accessories and attachments.

The bin in the bottom will hold over 150 pounds of sand. This nearly quadruples the weight of the stand, making it much more stable and helping to dampen vibrations of the saw attached to the top. The back right foot adjusts up or down so all four feet rest firmly on the floor.

Two important features help you see your scroll work. This stand is several inches higher than those that come with many commercial saws, raising the scroll saw's worktable to chest level. You don't have to stoop over to get a close view of the pattern lines. And there is a mount for a tension lamp that can be placed anywhere on the top of the stand to illuminate the work.

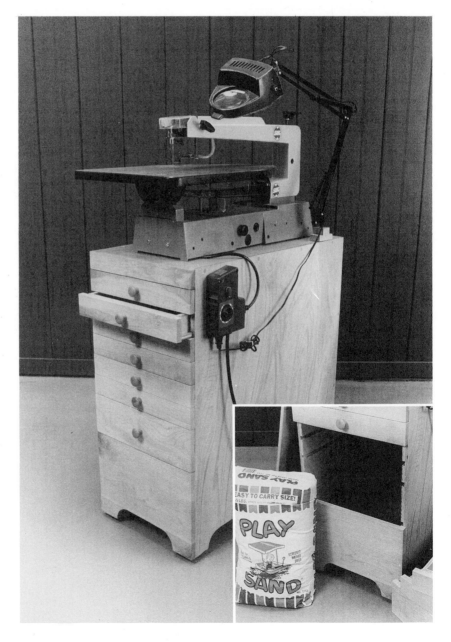

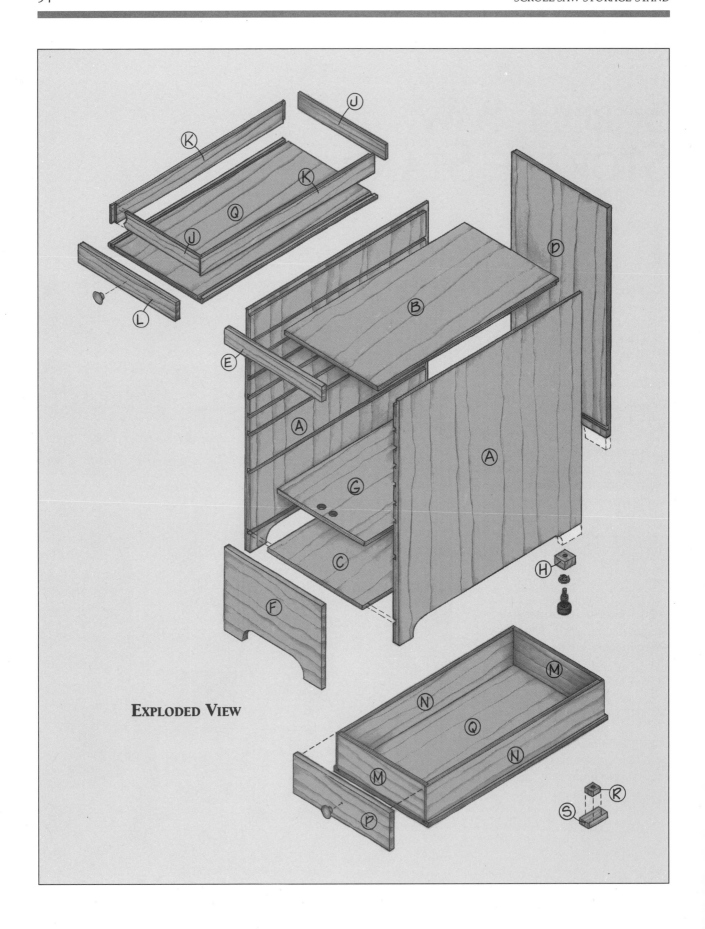

EXPLODED VIEW

MATERIALS LIST (FINISHED DIMENSIONS)

Parts

A. Sides (2) $^3/_4$" x 29$^1/_4$" x 33"
B. Top $^3/_4$" x 15$^1/_4$" x 29$^1/_4$"
C. Bottom $^1/_2$" x 15$^1/_4$" x 29$^1/_4$"
D. Back $^3/_4$" x 15$^1/_4$" x 32$^5/_8$"
E. Top trim* $^3/_4$" x 2" x 16"
F. Bin front* $^3/_4$" x 11" x 16"
G. Bin lid $^1/_2$" x 14$^7/_{16}$" x 28$^7/_{16}$"
H. Leveler block* 1" x 1$^1/_2$" x 1$^1/_2$"
J. Shallow drawer fronts/backs
    (12) $^1/_2$" x 1$^{15}/_{16}$" x 13$^{13}/_{16}$"
K. Shallow drawer
    sides (12) $^1/_2$" x 2$^3/_{16}$" x 28$^1/_4$"
L. Shallow drawer
    faces* (6) $^3/_4$" x 2$^7/_{16}$" x 16"
M. Deep drawer front/
    back (2) $^1/_2$" x 4$^7/_{16}$" x 13$^{13}/_{16}$"
N. Deep drawer
    sides (2) $^1/_2$" x 4$^{11}/_{16}$" x 28$^1/_4$"
P. Deep drawer
    face* $^3/_4$" x 4$^{15}/_{16}$" x 16"
Q. Drawer bottoms
    (7) $^1/_2$" x 15$^3/_{16}$" x 28$^1/_4$"
R. Lamp mount* $^3/_4$" x 1$^1/_2$" x 1$^1/_2$"
S. Lamp mount
    base* $^3/_4$" x 1$^1/_2$" x 3"

Hardware

#8 x 1$^1/_4$" Flathead wood screws
    (24–36)
4d Finishing nails ($^1/_4$ lb.)
$^3/_8$" Leveling foot
$^3/_8$" T-nut
1$^1/_4$" dia. Drawer pulls (7)

Make these parts from solid wood.

PLAN OF PROCEDURE

1 Select the stock and cut the parts to size.
To make this project, you'll need 5 board feet of 4/4 (four-quarters) hardwood lumber, a scrap of 6/4 (six-quarters) lumber, two-thirds sheet of $^3/_4$-inch plywood, and two-thirds sheet of $^1/_2$-inch plywood. The type of hardwood doesn't matter, as long as it's durable and matches the plywood veneer. All plywood should be cabinet grade or better. The scroll saw stand shown was made from hard maple and birch-veneered cabinet-grade plywood.

Plane the 4/4 stock to $^3/_4$ inch thick, and the 6/4 stock to 1 inch thick. Cut the parts to the sizes given in the Materials List, except for the drawer parts. Wait until after you've built the case to cut these.

2 Cut the joinery in the sides, top, back, and bin front. The parts of the stand case are assembled with rabbets and dadoes. Lay out and cut the joinery, using a router or a dado cutter:

■ $^3/_4$-inch-wide, $^3/_8$-inch-deep rabbets in the back edges of the sides to hold the back, as shown in the *Left Side Layout*
■ $^3/_4$-inch-wide, $^3/_8$-inch-deep rabbets in the top edges of the sides to hold the top
■ A $^3/_4$-inch-wide, $^3/_8$-inch-deep rabbet in the back edge of the top to fit over the back, as shown in the *Side View*
■ $^1/_2$-inch-wide, $^3/_8$-inch-deep dadoes in the sides to hold the bottom and the drawers
■ A $^1/_2$-inch-wide, $^3/_8$-inch-deep dado in the back to hold the bottom

■ $^1/_2$-inch-wide, $^3/_8$-inch-deep, 15$^1/_4$-inch-long double-blind dado in the bin front to hold the bottom
Note: Remember, the sides are *mirror images* of each other. Lay out and cut the joints on the right side so they are reversed from those shown in the *Left Side Layout*.

3 Cut the profiles of the sides, back, and bin front. Lay out the profiles of the feet on the sides, back, and bin front. Note that where the back and the right side come together, the foot is cut 1$^1/_2$ inches shorter than the other three feet. This allows the adjustable *leveling foot* to work.

Cut the profiles with a saber saw and sand the cut edges. To save time, stack the two sides and hold them together with double-faced carpet tape. Do the same for the back and the bin front. Stack the parts with their inside faces together and make sure the bottom edges of the parts are flush. Cut and sand the shapes of the feet with the parts stacked. Take the stacks apart, and cut short the right foot on the back and the back foot on the right side.

4 Drill holes in the bin lid. The bin lid fits inside the bin to cover the sand. In case you need to lift the bin lid after you shovel the sand in place, drill two 1-inch-diameter finger holes near the front edge, as shown in the *Bin Lid Detail*.

5 Assemble the case. Finish sand the parts of the case. Assemble the sides, back, top, and bottom

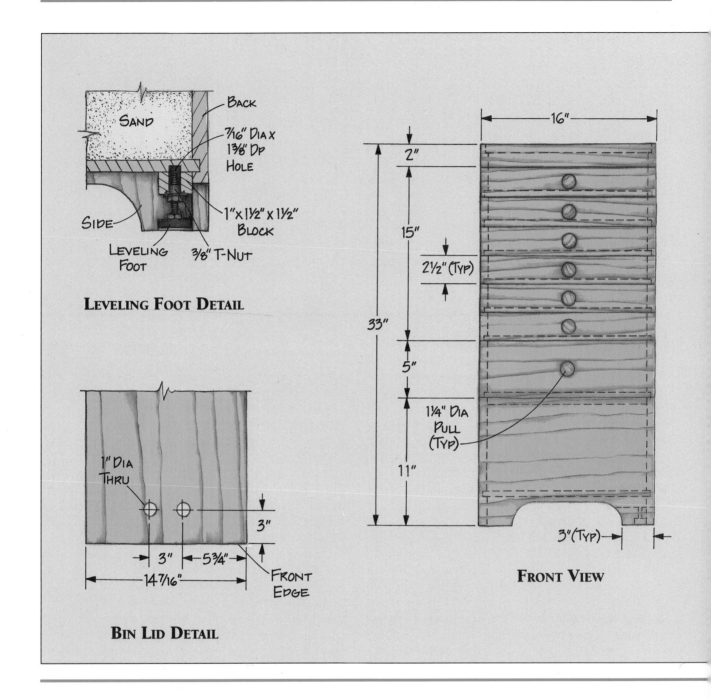

LEVELING FOOT DETAIL

SAND

BACK

7/16" DIA X
1 3/8" DP
HOLE

SIDE

1" x 1 1/2" x 1 1/2"
BLOCK

LEVELING
FOOT

3/8" T-NUT

BIN LID DETAIL

1" DIA
THRU

3"

3"   5 3/4"

14 7/16"

FRONT
EDGE

16"

2"

15"

2 1/2" (TYP)

5"

1 1/4" DIA
PULL
(TYP)

33"

11"

3" (TYP)

FRONT VIEW

with glue and reinforce the joints with flathead wood screws. Then attach the top trim and the bin front with glue and screws. Counterbore and countersink all screws, then cover the heads with wooden plugs. Sand the plugs flush with the surrounding surface.

Glue the leveler block to the bottom, in the right back corner. Let the glue dry, then drill a 7/16-inch-diameter, 1 3/8-inch-deep hole through the center of the block and partway into the bottom. Install a T-nut and the leveling foot, as shown in the *Leveling Foot Detail*.

Glue the lamp mount to the lamp mount base, as shown in the *Lamp Mount Detail*. Let the glue dry and drill a hole through both parts to fit the base of your tension lamp. (Most lamps require a 1/2-inch-diameter hole, but it's wise to measure before you drill.) *Don't* fasten the mount assembly to the case yet; wait until after you've installed the scroll saw.

6 Cut the drawer parts to size. No matter how carefully you work, the size of a case sometimes changes

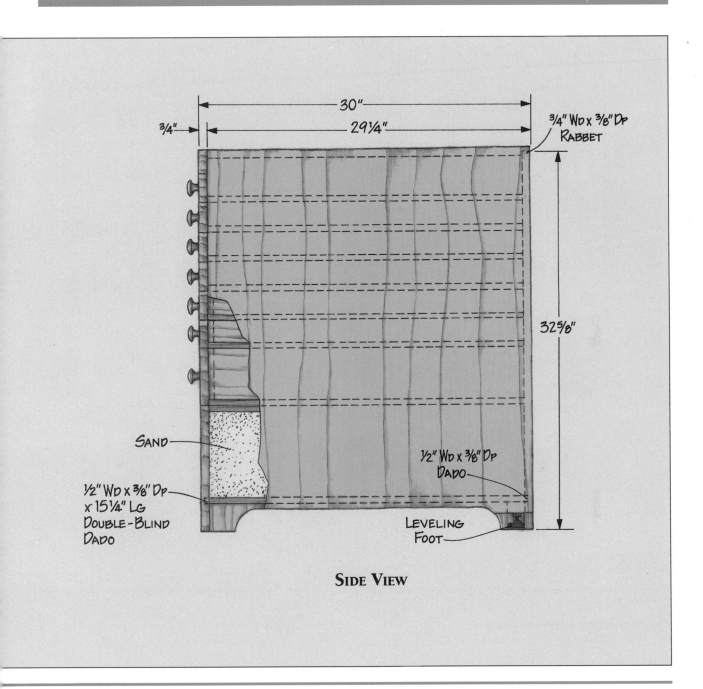

30"

3/4"

29¼"

3/4" Wd x 3/8" Dp
Rabbet

32⅝"

Sand

½" Wd x 3/8" Dp
Dado

½" Wd x 3/8" Dp
x 15¼" Lg
Double-Blind
Dado

Leveling
Foot

Side View

as you build it. For this reason, it's best to wait until after you've assembled the case before cutting the drawer parts.

Measure the width of the opening in the front of the case. If it varies from what is shown in the drawings, adjust the sizes of the drawer parts to compensate. Then cut the drawer parts to size. **Note:** The completed drawers should be ¹/₁₆ to ¹/₈ inch *narrower* than the opening to work properly. Remember this when figuring the sizes.

7 Cut the drawer joinery. Like the case, the drawers are assembled with simple rabbets and dadoes. Cut these joints:

■ ½-inch-wide, ¹/₄-inch-deep rabbets in the front and back ends of the drawer sides, as shown in the *All Drawers/Top View*

■ ½-inch-wide, ¹/₄-inch-deep dadoes in the drawer bottoms to hold the sides, as shown in the *Shallow Drawer/Front View*

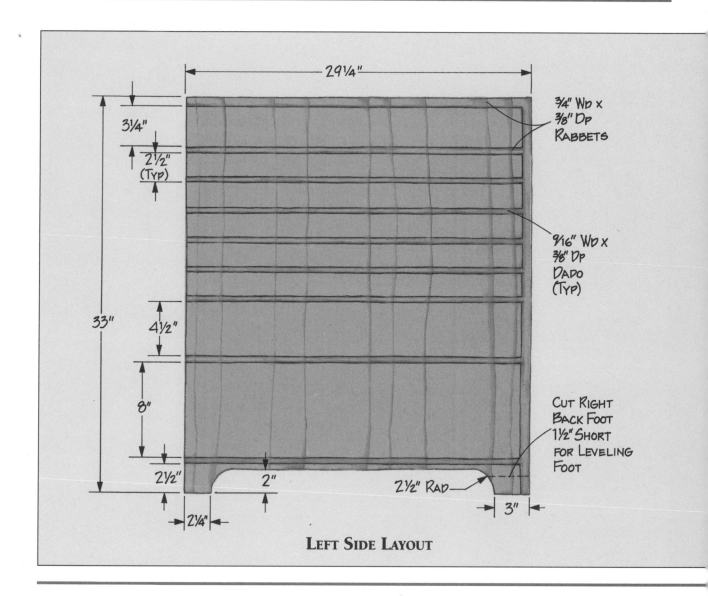

LEFT SIDE LAYOUT

8 Assemble and fit the drawers. Lightly sand the drawer parts. Glue the drawer fronts, backs, sides, and bottoms together. Reinforce the glue joints with finishing nails. Set the heads of the nails below the wood surface. Do *not* glue the drawer faces to the fronts yet.

Slide the drawers into the case, fitting the drawer bottoms into the 1/2-inch-wide dadoes in the sides. If any of the drawers bind in the case, sand or scrape the bottoms until they slide in and out easily.

Lay the case on its back and place scraps of 1/4-inch plywood on the inside surface of the back, near the corners, to serve as spacers. Slide the drawers all the way into the case — the spacers should hold the drawer fronts flush with the front edges of the case. Place the drawer faces over the fronts, fitting them so

there's a 1/32- to 1/16-inch gap between them. Temporarily attach the faces to the case with carpet tape; then drill 1/8-inch-diameter pilot holes through the faces *and* the fronts where you will later attach drawer pulls.

Remove the drawer faces and discard the tape. Spread glue on the drawer fronts, and lay the faces back in place. Temporarily drive #8 flathead wood screws through the pilot holes in the faces and into the fronts — this will hold the faces in place until you can apply the clamps. Remove the drawers from the case and clamp the faces to the drawer fronts. Let the glue dry, then back the screws out of the pilot holes. Enlarge the holes and mount drawer pulls.

9 Finish the scroll saw stand. Remove the drawers from the case. Do any necessary finish

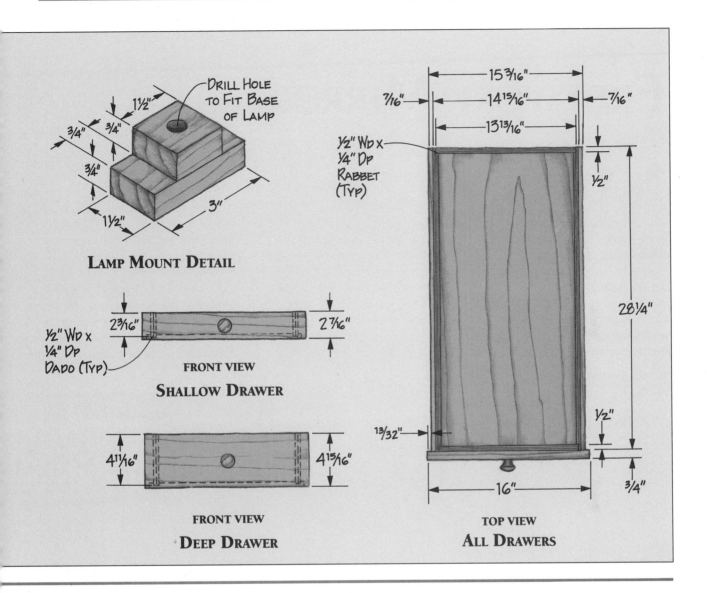

DRILL HOLE
TO FIT BASE
OF LAMP

1½"

¾" ¾"

¾"

1½"

3"

LAMP MOUNT DETAIL

½" WD x
¼" DP
DADO (TYP)

2³⁄₁₆" 2⁷⁄₁₆"

FRONT VIEW
SHALLOW DRAWER

4¹¹⁄₁₆" 4¹⁵⁄₁₆"

FRONT VIEW
DEEP DRAWER

15³⁄₁₆"

7⁄₁₆" 14¹⁵⁄₁₆" 7⁄₁₆"

13¹³⁄₁₆"

½" WD x
¼" DP
RABBET
(TYP)

½"

28¼"

13⁄₃₂"

½"

16"

¾"

TOP VIEW
ALL DRAWERS

sanding and apply several coats of tung oil or Danish oil, letting each coat dry thoroughly before applying another. Rub out the last coat with #0000 steel wool and paste wax — the wax will help the finish resist spills and other abuse. Also wax the drawer bottoms and the dadoes that hold them to help the drawers slide smoothly. Replace the drawers in the case.

10 Install the scroll saw and lamp mount.
Remove your scroll saw from its commercial stand and position it on the top of the storage stand. Mark for bolt holes, drill them, then bolt the saw to the top. If necessary, remove the switch from the commercial stand and fasten it to the storage stand in a convenient location. **Note:** The scroll saw *must* be securely fas-

tened to the top of the stand, not only for safety but to reduce vibration.

With the saw in place, determine where the lamp should be placed. Fasten the lamp mount to the top with flathead wood screws. Do *not* glue it in place, in case you want to move it later.

Move the saw and the stand to where you will use the scroll saw. Adjust the leveling foot so all four feet rest solidly on the floor and the stand doesn't rock. Remove the drawers and fill the bin with dry sand. (Use packaged "play sand," sold for sandboxes at most building supply stores.) Rest the bin lid on the sand and replace the drawers. Lastly, insert the lamp into the lamp mount.

8

Fretwork Mirror

Mirrors with fancy fretwork frames have been popular since before the invention of scroll saws. The intricate patterns were copied from stylized cloud forms used by old-time Japanese artists and craftsmen. English cabinetmakers initially saw them on furniture imported from the Orient in the early eighteenth century. The style caught on, and American craftsmen were soon copying their English counterparts, at first cutting the cloud forms with hand-held fretsaws, then later with mechanical scroll saws.

Although this mirror appears to be complex, it's an extremely simple project to build. The frame is constructed like an ordinary picture frame, with mitered corners and a rabbet to hold the mirror. The corner joints are splined at the corners for strength. The fretwork is cut on a scroll saw, then fitted to blind grooves in the outside edges of the frame.

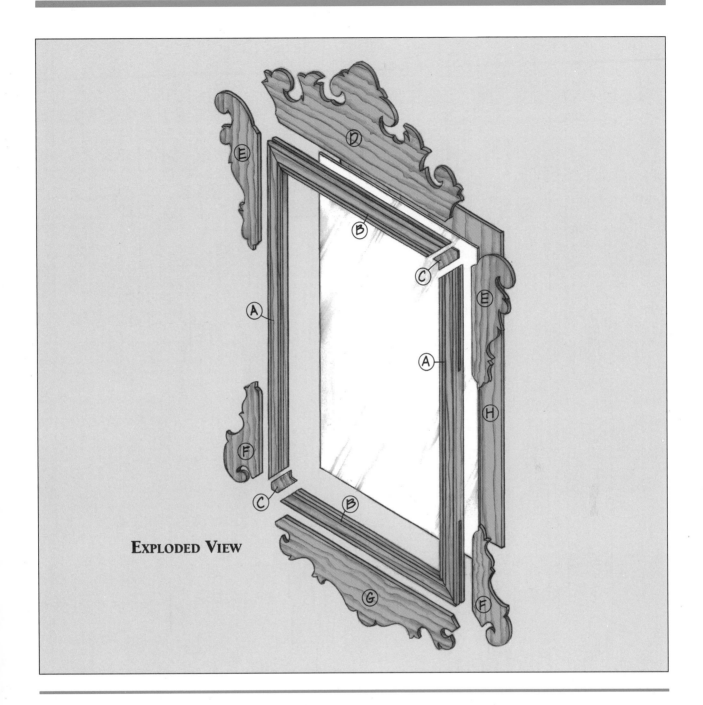

EXPLODED VIEW

MATERIALS LIST (FINISHED DIMENSIONS)

Parts

A. Stiles (2) $3/4'' \times 1^1/2'' \times 27''$
B. Rails (2) $3/4'' \times 1^1/2'' \times 17''$
C. Splines (4) $1/4'' \times 1'' \times 2^1/4''$
D. Top
    fretwork $1/4'' \times 8^1/4'' \times 19^1/4''$
E. Top side
    fretwork (2) $1/4'' \times 4'' \times 11^1/2''$

F. Bottom side
    fretwork (2) $1/4'' \times 3^1/2'' \times 8^3/4''$
G. Bottom
    fretwork $1/4'' \times 4^3/4'' \times 17^1/2''$
H. Back* $1/4'' \times 14^3/4'' \times 24^3/4''$

*Make this part from plywood or
hardboard.

Hardware

$3/4''$ Wire brads (8–12)
$1/8'' \times 14^5/8'' \times 24^5/8''$ Mirror
$1/4''$ Eye screws (2)
30# Picture wire (18")

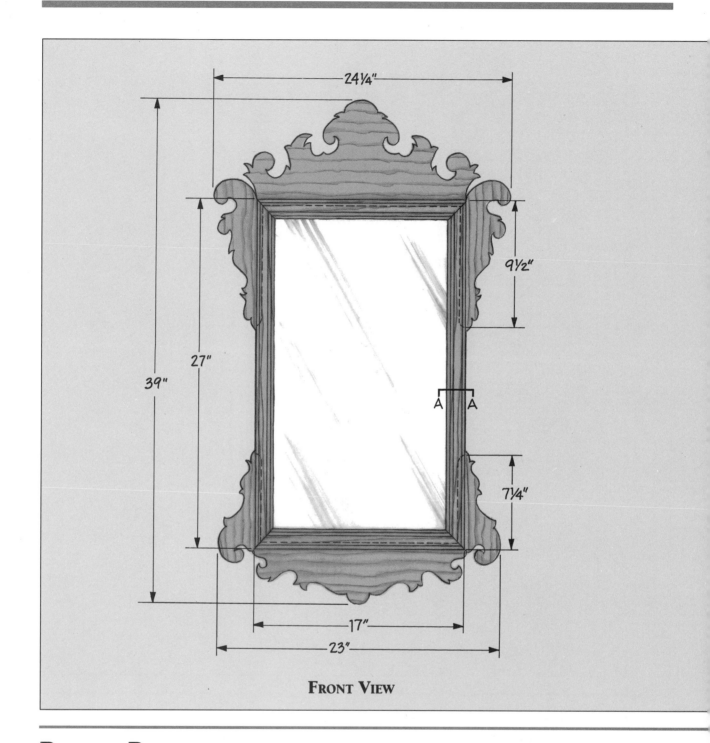

FRONT VIEW

PLAN OF PROCEDURE

1 **Select and prepare the stock.** To make this project, you need approximately 6 board feet of 4/4 (four-quarters) hardwood lumber. You can use almost any hardwood, although traditionally these mirrors were built from mahogany, cherry, walnut, and maple. The mirror shown is built from quilted maple.

To prepare the stock, first rip enough 1³⁄₄-inch-wide strips from the rough lumber to make the frame. Resaw the remaining stock in half. Plane the strips to ³⁄₄ inch thick and 1¹⁄₂ inches wide. Plane the resawed boards to ¹⁄₄ inch thick.

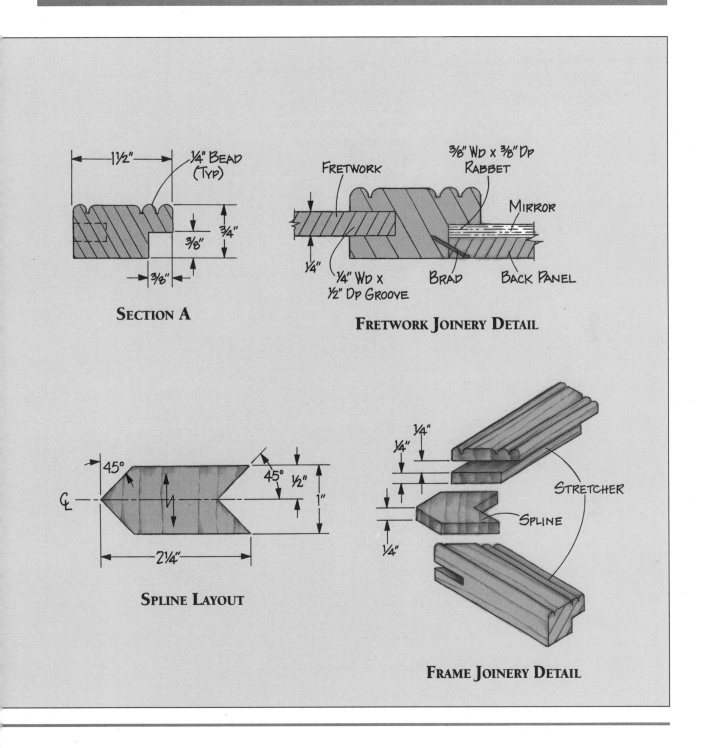

SECTION A

FRETWORK JOINERY DETAIL

SPLINE LAYOUT

FRAME JOINERY DETAIL

2 **Shape the frame stock.** The rails and stiles have small, decorative beads on the front faces and rabbets in the back faces, as shown in *Section A.* Cut the beads with a table-mounted router and a point-cut roundover bit, a shaper and a beading cutter, or a molding head and a set of beading knives. Cut the ³/8-

inch-wide, ³/8-inch-deep rabbet with a router and a straight bit or with a dado cutter.

3 **Assemble the frame.** Finish sand the frame stock, smoothing the beads. Cut the rails and stiles to length, mitering the ends at 45 degrees.

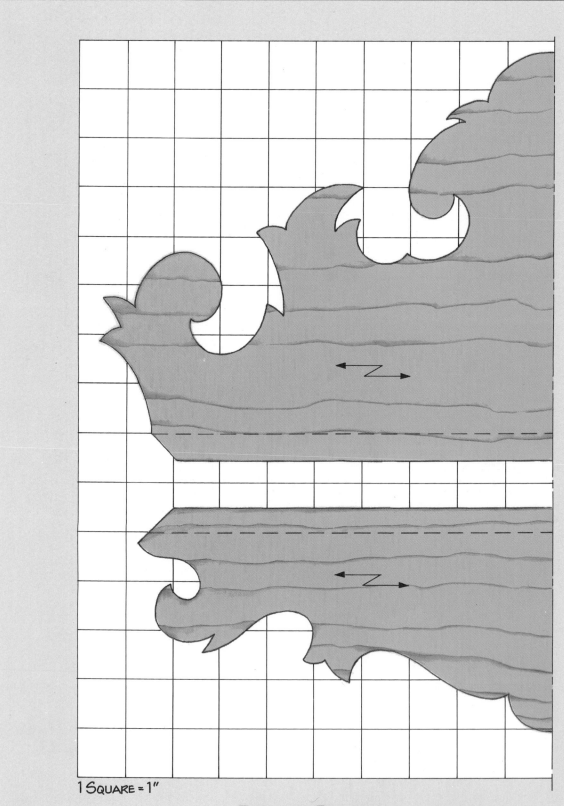

1 SQUARE = 1"

FRETWORK PATTERNS

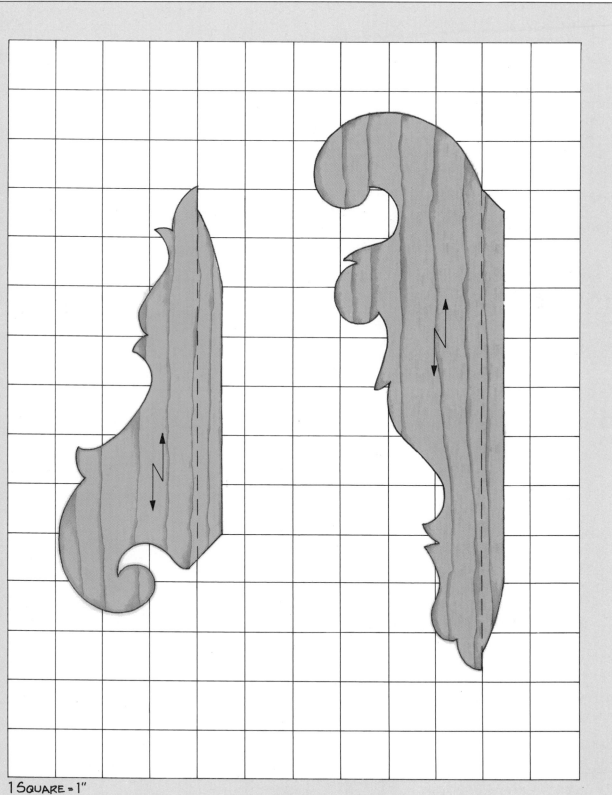

1 SQUARE = 1"

FRETWORK PATTERNS

Using a table-mounted router or a dado cutter, make ¼-inch-wide, ½-inch-deep grooves in the mitered ends for splines, as shown in the *Frame Joinery Detail.* Cut four splines from the ¼-inch-thick stock. Note that the wood grain of each spline must run side to side, as shown in the *Spline Layout,* in order to cross the miter joint and reinforce it. If the grain runs end to end, parallel to the joint, the spline will provide no reinforcement.

Test fit the rails, stiles, and splines. If the fit is satisfactory, assemble the frame with glue.

A SAFETY REMINDER

It's essential that you reinforce the miter joints with splines so they won't come apart when the assembled frame is machined.

---

4 Cut the fretwork. Enlarge the *Fretwork Patterns* and trace them on the ¼-inch-thick stock. Pay careful attention to the grain direction of each pattern. Cut the patterns with a scroll saw. Pad-saw the side fretwork to save time.

5 Cut the grooves in the frame. Sand the miter joints on the frame so the wood surfaces are clean and flush. Using a table-mounted router or a dado

cutter, plow ¼-inch-wide, ½-inch-deep grooves in the rails. These grooves must be perfectly centered in the edge of the frame — ¼ inch from each face.

The grooves in the stiles are blind at one end, as shown in the *Front View.* To cut the grooves near the *bottom* ends of the stiles, clamp a block to the fence to stop the cut when it's 7¼ inches long. Readjust the block so it stops the cut when it's 9½ inches long, and cut the grooves near the *top* ends.

6 Glue the fretwork to the frame. Test fit the fretwork in the frame. When you're sure that the parts fit properly, finish sand the frame and the fretwork. Glue the fretwork in the grooves. (SEE FIGURE 8-1.)

7 Finish the completed fretwork frame. Do any necessary touch-up sanding and apply a finish. Traditionally, these frames were finished with lacquer, shellac, or hand-rubbed oil, but you can use any clear finish. The frame shown is finished with sprayed polyurethane.

8 Install the mirror. Lay the mirror in place and fit the back over it. Secure the mirror and the back in the frame with small brads. Install an eye screw in each stile, several inches from the top of the frame. Run 30-pound picture wire between the eyes to hang the completed mirror.

8-1 Because the fretwork is uniquely shaped, it's almost impossible to secure it to the frame with ordinary clamps during assembly. Instead, use masking tape to clamp the fretwork in the grooves, stretching the tape as tight as possible without tearing it. The masking tape is slightly elastic and will apply enough pressure to create a strong glue bond.

9

VICTORIAN DISPLAY SHELVES

When open fretwork was introduced to America in the late nineteenth century, craftsmen in the United States, true to their national character, searched for something *practical* they could make with this purely decorative art form. One of the most popular applications was small shelving units, such as these corner display shelves with lacelike supports. These became commonplace during the Victorian period.

The openwork patterns decrease the innate strength of the wood — the grain is no longer continuous, because the interior cuts interrupt it in so many spots. Consequently, the supports for these shelves are considerably weaker than they might be. But the shelves are intended to display knickknacks and other lightweight pieces — not heavy items.

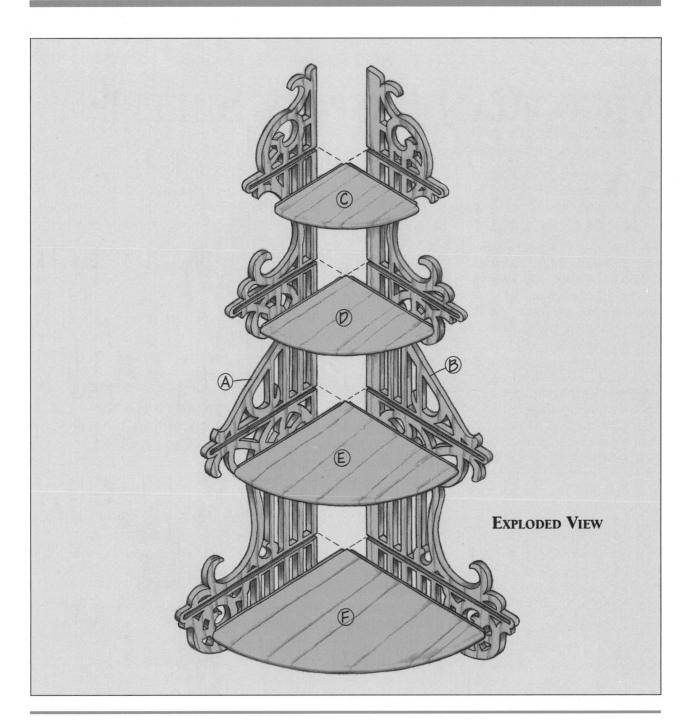

EXPLODED VIEW

MATERIALS LIST (FINISHED DIMENSIONS)

Parts

A. Narrow
   support $^3/_8''$ x $8^3/_4''$ x $34^1/_2''$

B. Wide
   support $^3/_8''$ x $9^1/_8''$ x $34^1/_2''$

C. Top shelf $^3/_8''$ x $4^1/_2''$ x $4^1/_2''$

D. Upper middle
   shelf $^3/_8''$ x $5^3/_4''$ x $5^3/_4''$

E. Lower middle
   shelf $^3/_8''$ x $7^1/_4''$ x $7^1/_4''$

F. Bottom
   shelf $^3/_8''$ x $8^7/_8''$ x $8^7/_8''$

Hardware

#6 x $^3/_4''$ Flathead wood screws (12)

PLAN OF PROCEDURE

1 Select the stock and cut the parts to size.
To make this project, you need approximately 5 board feet of 4/4 (four-quarters) hardwood lumber. You can use any closed-grain or medium-grain hardwood; the corner shelves shown are made from mahogany.

Resaw the lumber in half and plane each half to ³⁄₈ inch thick. Cut the parts to the sizes specified in the Materials List.

2 Cut the dadoes in the supports. The shelves rest in ¹⁄₄-inch-wide, ¹⁄₄-inch-deep dadoes in the supports. The dadoes are *blind* — stopped near the front edge so they won't be seen when the shelves are assembled. Enlarge the *Support Pattern* and use it to lay out the dadoes on both supports. Cut the dadoes

with a hand-held router. (*SEE FIGURE 9-1.*) **Note:** Make the blind dadoes in the narrow support ³⁄₈ inch shorter than those in the wide support.

3 Cut the tenons in the shelves. The sides of the shelves that join the supports are rabbeted on both faces to fit in the dadoes. These rabbets create ¹⁄₄-inch-thick tenons. Using a table-mounted router or a dado cutter, cut ¹⁄₄-inch-wide, ¹⁄₁₆-inch-deep rabbets in one end and one edge of each shelf. Rabbet both faces, as shown in the *Shelf Joinery Detail/Front View.*

4 Cut the profile of the shelves and shape the edges. Lay out the curved edge of the shelves, as shown in the *Top View,* and the notches in the front

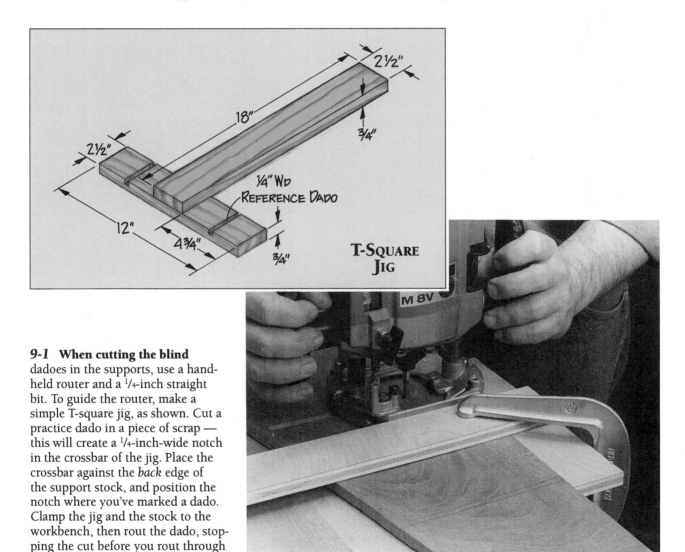

9-1 When cutting the blind dadoes in the supports, use a hand-held router and a ¹⁄₄-inch straight bit. To guide the router, make a simple T-square jig, as shown. Cut a practice dado in a piece of scrap — this will create a ¹⁄₄-inch-wide notch in the crossbar of the jig. Place the crossbar against the *back* edge of the support stock, and position the notch where you've marked a dado. Clamp the jig and the stock to the workbench, then rout the dado, stopping the cut before you rout through to the front edge. Repeat for each dado.

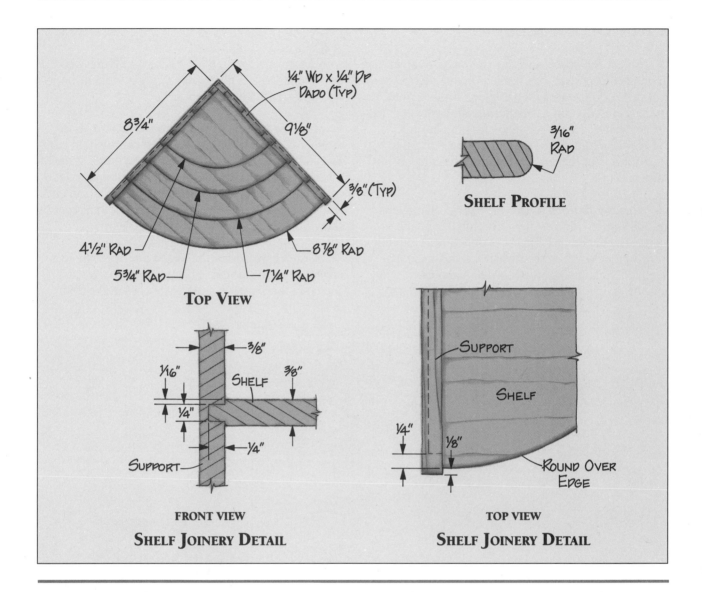

corners, as shown in the *Shelf Joinery Detail/Top View*. Cut the notches and curved edges on a scroll saw. Round over the curved edges with a file or rasp, as shown in the *Shelf Profile*.

Fit the shelves to the dadoes in the supports. If the fit is too tight or too loose, make the necessary corrections now, *before* you cut the openwork pattern. Once you cut the openwork, the supports will be more delicate and may break if there's a lot of fitting still to do.

5 **Cut the openwork patterns.** Stack the sides face to face, holding the stack together with double-faced carpet tape. Make sure the back edge of the narrow support is ³/₈ inch from the back edge of the wide support and parallel to it. Affix the pattern to the exposed face of the narrow support with spray adhesive.

Drill the necessary saw gates and cut the pattern on a scroll saw, using a spiral blade. Afterwards, separate the supports and discard the tape.

6 **Assemble the supports and shelves.** Finish sand the supports and the shelves. Sand only the faces of the supports; you shouldn't have to sand the sawed edges, because the scroll saw blade will have left them reasonably smooth. Assemble the shelves and supports with glue and screws.

7 **Finish the shelving unit.** After the glue dries, do any necessary touch-up sanding on the completed corner shelves. Apply several coats of a clear finish. The shelves shown were sprayed with acrylic (water-based lacquer).

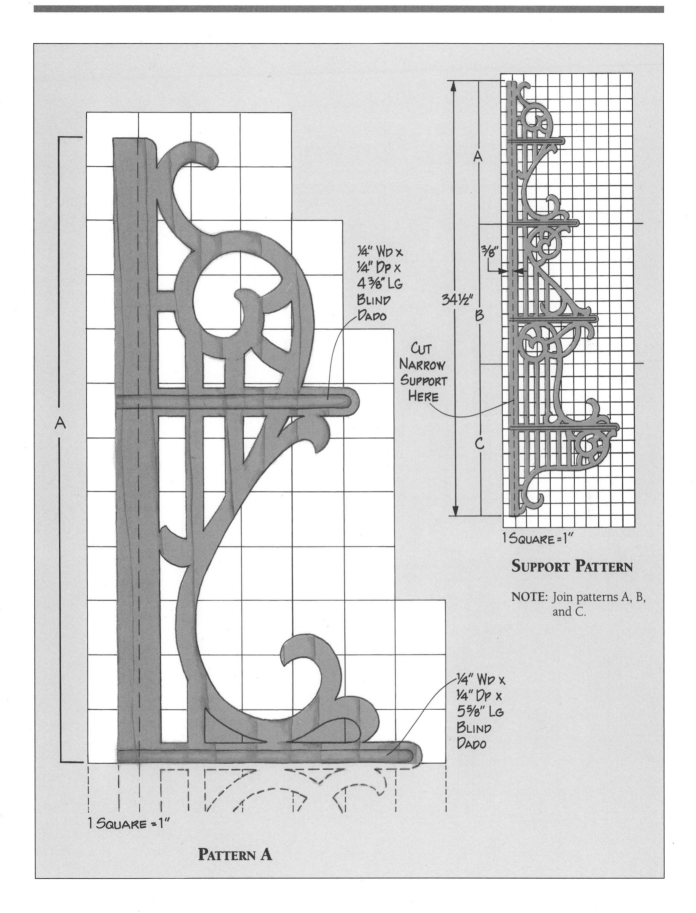

¼" WD x
¼" DP x
4 ⅜" LG
BLIND
DADO

CUT
NARROW
SUPPORT
HERE

¼" WD x
¼" DP x
5 ⅝" LG
BLIND
DADO

1 SQUARE = 1"

PATTERN A

34½"

A

B

C

⅜"

A

1 SQUARE = 1"

SUPPORT PATTERN

NOTE: Join patterns A, B, and C.

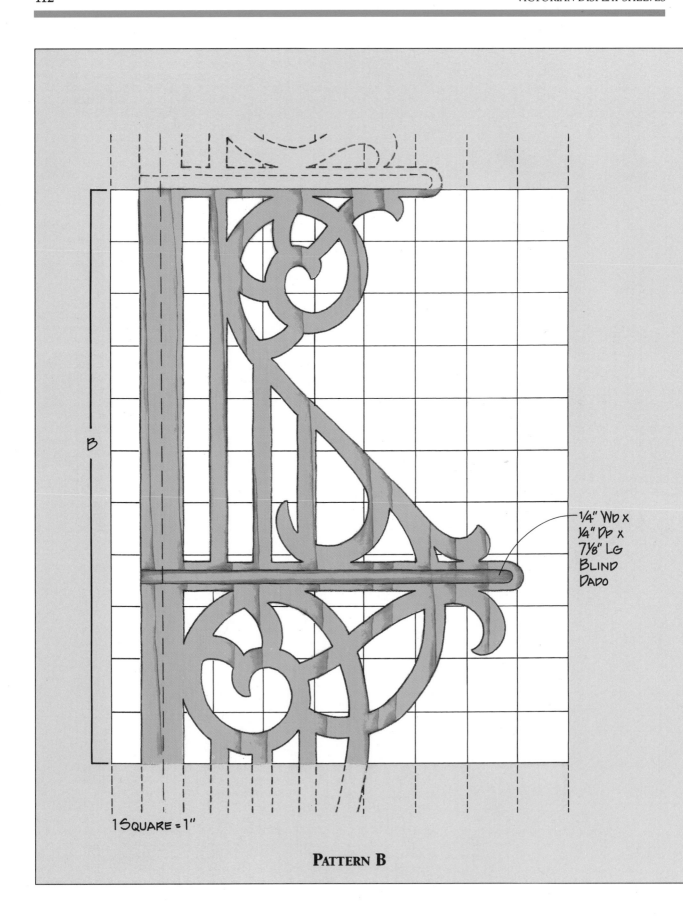

1/4" Wᴅ x
1/4" Dᴘ x
7 1/8" Lɢ
Bʟɪɴᴅ
Dᴀᴅᴏ

B

1 Sǫᴜᴀʀᴇ = 1"

Pᴀᴛᴛᴇʀɴ B

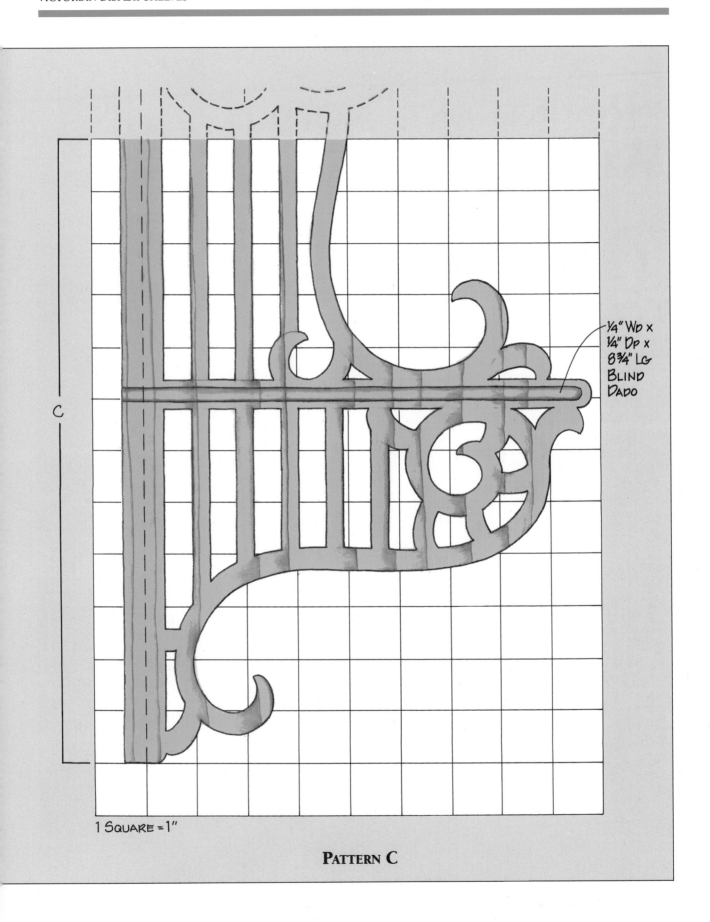

¼" Wd x
¼" Dp x
8¾" Lg
Blind
Dado

C

1 Square = 1"

PATTERN C

10

"ROUND AND ROUND" WHIRLIGIG

This clever whirligig by folk artist Mary Jane Favorite portrays a whimsical chase scene: A woman chases a dog who chases a cat who chases a mouse who chases the woman...and so on, round and round. The wind-powered mechanism used to perpetuate this chase is unique, another one of Mary Jane's creations. This is, as far as she knows, the first whirligig to use a "wind wheel" device.

The device works something like a waterwheel. The wind blows against the paddles, which are attached to the wheel. A wind vane points a wind shield into the wind so the paddles on one side of the wheel are protected from the wind, while those on the other side are exposed to it. There is more wind pressure on the exposed side than on the protected side, and this causes the wheel to turn. The woman, dog, cat, and mouse, which are mounted on the wheel, chase each other round and round.

EXPLODED VIEW

MATERIALS LIST (FINISHED DIMENSIONS)

Parts

A.	Wheel	10" dia. x ½"	D. Woman	⅜" x 8" x 9¾"	H. Woman's dowel	¼" dia. x 3"
B.	Collar	2" dia. x ½"	E. Dog	⅜" x 4¼" x 7½"	J. Dog's dowel	¼" dia. x 2¼"
C.	Paddles*		F. Cat	⅜" x 2½" x 6½"	K. Cat's dowel	¼" dia. x 2"
	(16)	⅛" x 3½" x 3½"	G. Mouse	⅜" x 1¼" x 2½"	L. Mouse's dowel	¼" dia. x 1½"

(continued) ▷

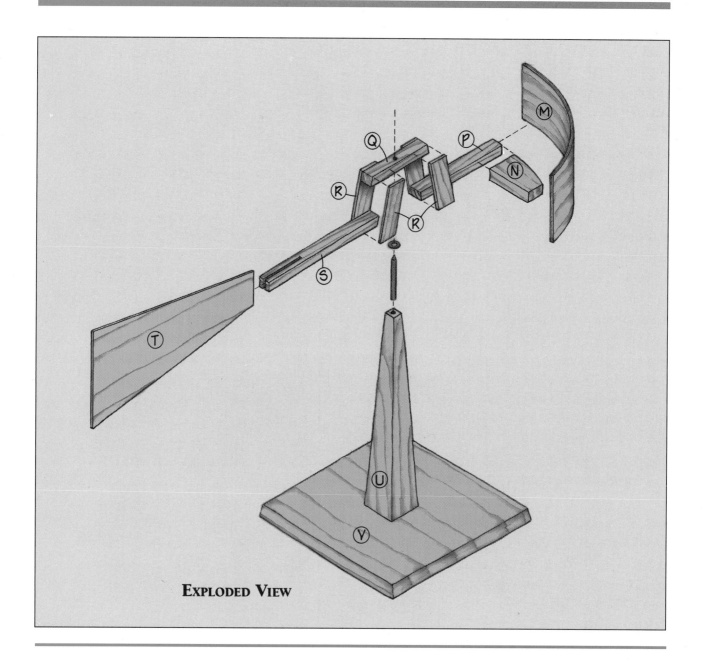

EXPLODED VIEW

MATERIALS LIST — CONTINUED

Parts

M.	Wind shield*	1/8" x 4" x 12"	T.	Wind vane*	1/8" x 6" x 12"	
N.	Wind shield brace	1/2" x 2" x 2 3/4"	U.	Post†	2" x 2" x 12"	
P.	Wind shield support	1/2" x 3/4" x 5 3/4"	V.	Base†	3/4" x 10" x 10"	
Q.	Wind vane pivot	1/2" x 3/4" x 4"				
R.	Gussets (4)	1/8" x 1" x 3 1/2"				
S.	Wind vane support	1/2" x 3/4" x 8 3/8"				

*Make these parts from plywood or glue up four layers of veneer to make your own plywood.
†Optional — for indoor display only.

Hardware

20d Nail
1/4" I.D. x 11/16" Pipe
1/4" dia. x 2 1/2" Steel rod
1/4" Flat washer
1/4" Fender washers (12–24)
#10 x 2 1/2" Flathead wood screws (2)
#10 x 3/4" Roundhead wood screws (2–3)
14-gauge Copper wire (6")

PLAN OF PROCEDURE

1 Select the stock and cut the parts to size. To make this project, you need about 2 board feet of 4/4 (four-quarters) hardwood lumber and 3 square feet of veneer. If the whirligig will be used outside, use a weather-resistant wood such as mahogany or white cedar (also known as juniper). If you're going to display this whirligig indoors, you need an additional board foot of 4/4 stock for the base and a 2-inch turning blank 12 inches long for the post. Indoors, you can use any hardwood, or even mix hardwoods. You can also substitute ⅛-inch Baltic birch plywood for the paddles and the wind vane. The indoor whirligig shown is made from poplar, maple veneer, and Baltic birch plywood.

Plane a single board foot of the 4/4 stock to ¾ inch thick and cut the base. Plane another board foot to ½ inch thick and cut the wheel, collar, pivot, and supports. Resaw the remaining board foot, plane the pieces to ⅜ inch thick, and cut the pieces for the figures — woman, dog, cat, and mouse. Plane and joint the turning blank square.

To make the ⅛-inch-thick parts, laminate four layers of veneer face to face, alternating the grain direction of each layer to make plywood. Use a waterproof glue, such as epoxy or resorcinol, if the whirligig will be used outdoors. To make the curved wind shield, press the veneers in a bending form while the glue dries. (*SEE FIGURE 10-1.*) Cut and trim the plywood.

2 Cut and drill the figures, wheel, and collar. Enlarge the *Figure Patterns* and trace them on the stock. Lay out the wheel and the collar. Drill a ¼-inch-diameter hole, ¼ inch deep in the center of the wheel, and a ¼-inch-diameter hole through the center of the collar. Cut the profiles on a scroll saw, and sand the wheel and the collar perfectly round. (*SEE FIGURE 10-2.*) Drill ¼-inch-diameter holes approximately ¾ inch deep in the bottom edges of the figures, and ¼-inch-diameter holes ⅛ inch deep in the top surface of the wheel, as shown in the *Figure Mounting Layout*. Also drill ³⁄₃₂-inch-diameter, ¼-inch-deep holes in the body of the mouse where you will insert the wires to make the legs and tail.

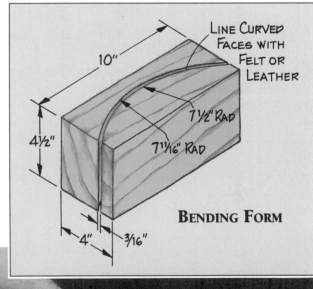

10-1 To make the curved wind shield, you must first make a bending form. Laminate six layers of ¾-inch particleboard to make a block 4½ inches thick, 4 inches wide, and 10 inches long. Cut the form in three pieces, sawing a 7½-inch radius and a 7¹¹⁄₁₆-inch radius. Discard the middle piece and line the curved faces of the remaining two with felt or leather. Glue four layers of veneer face to face, alternating the grain direction of each layer, and clamp the veneers in the form while the glue is still wet. Let the glue dry overnight, then remove the curved lamination. Trim and sand the ends and edges.

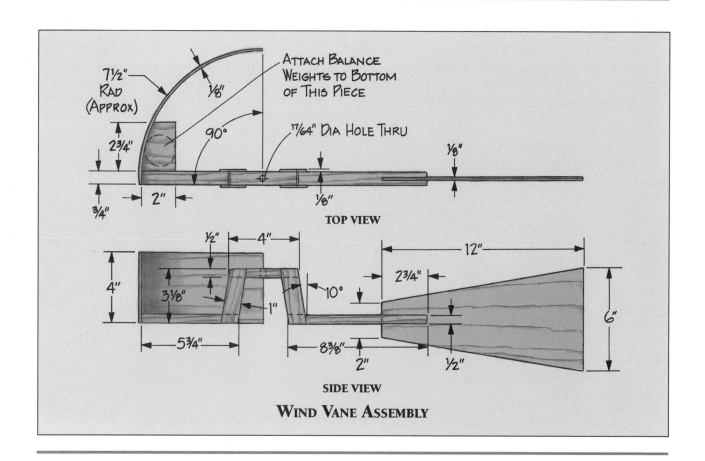

TOP VIEW

SIDE VIEW

WIND VANE ASSEMBLY

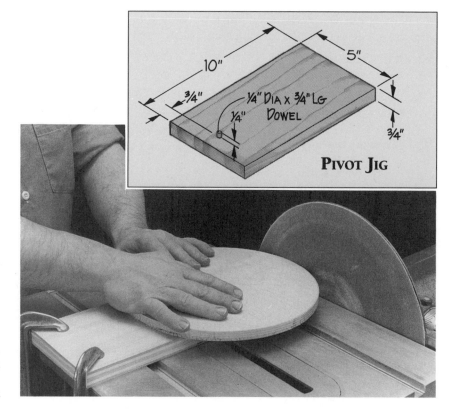

PIVOT JIG

10-2 **After sawing the profiles of** the wheel and collar, sand them perfectly round. Make the pivot jig shown and clamp it to the table of a disc sander. Place the wheel on the jig so the hole in the center fits over the pivot. Adjust the position of the jig so the edge of the wheel just kisses the sanding disc. Turn on the sander and slowly spin the wheel. Turn off the sander, adjust the wheel a little closer, and sand again. Repeat until the wheel has no flat spots on the edges. Do the same for the collar.

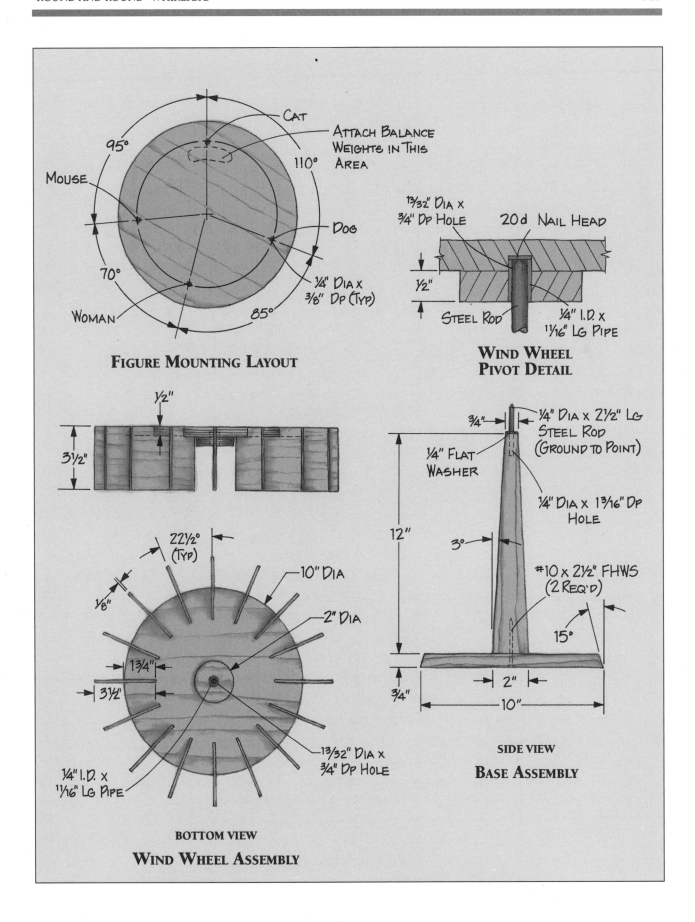

FIGURE MOUNTING LAYOUT

WIND WHEEL PIVOT DETAIL

WIND WHEEL ASSEMBLY
BOTTOM VIEW

BASE ASSEMBLY
SIDE VIEW

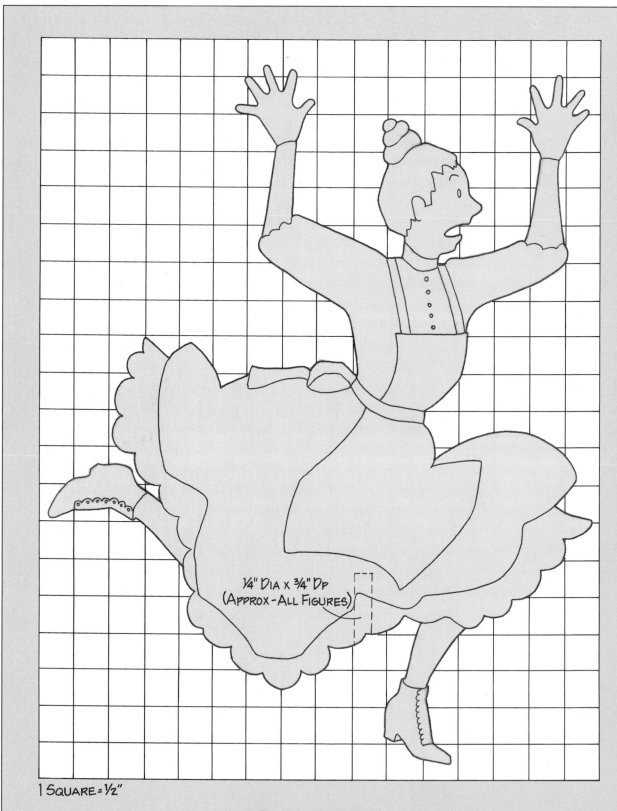

¼" Dia x ¾" Dp
(Approx - All Figures)

1 Square = ½"

Figure Pattern

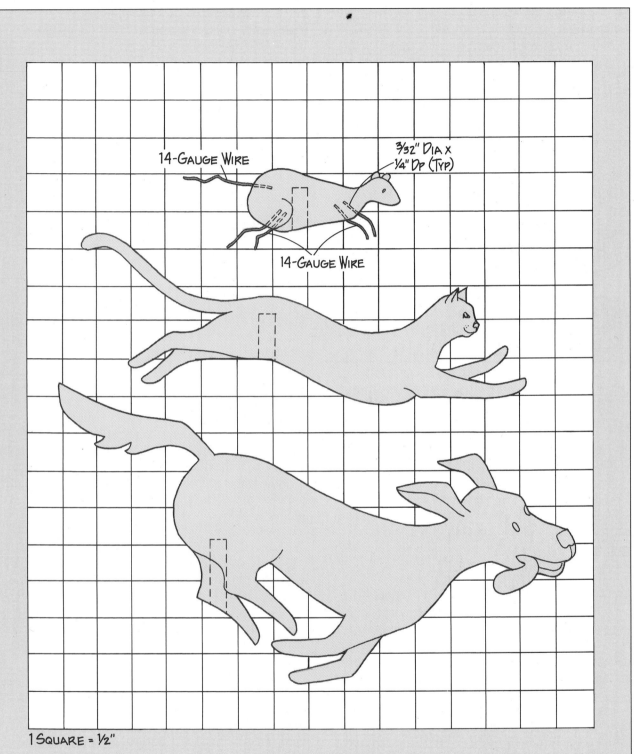

14-GAUGE WIRE

³⁄₃₂" DIA X
¹⁄₄" DP (TYP)

14-GAUGE WIRE

1 SQUARE = ½"

FIGURE PATTERNS

NOTE: Use ³⁄₈" thick stock.

3 Assemble the wind wheel. Lay out the slots for the paddles around the circumference of the wheel, as shown in the *Wind Wheel Assembly/Bottom View.* Cut the slots with a scroll saw.

Finish sand the paddles, wheel, and collar. Glue the wheel and the collar together, using the ¼-inch-diameter steel pivot rod to keep the center of the parts aligned. When the glue dries, remove the rod and enlarge the center holes, drilling a single hole ¹³/₃₂ inch in diameter and ¾ inch deep, as shown in the *Wind Wheel Pivot Detail.* Cut the head from a 20d nail and drop it into the hole, then press the ¼-inch-I.D. pipe into the hole atop the nail head.

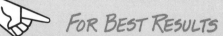

FOR BEST RESULTS

More than likely, the inside diameter of the pipe will be a bit *undersize.* Before you press it in place, ream it out with a ¼-inch-diameter drill bit. Make sure the pivot rod fits it loosely. If not, ream it out with a ¹⁷/₆₄-inch-diameter bit.

Glue the paddles in the slots. Make sure the top edges of the paddles are flush with the top surface of the wheel.

4 Assemble the wind vane. Lay out the profiles of the wind vane, gussets, and wind shield brace. Cut the profiles and miter the ends of the supports and pivot, as shown in the *Wind Vane Assembly/Side View.* Drill a ¹⁷/₆₄-inch-diameter hole through the pivot and cut a ⅛-inch-wide, 2¾-inch-long slot in the wind vane support. Finish sand the parts of the wind vane assembly and glue them together.

5 Make the base. If you've elected to make the base, drill a ¼-diameter hole 1³/₁₆ inches deep in the top end of the post. Taper the post on all four sides, as shown in the *Base Assembly/Side View,* and bevel the ends and edges of the base. Finish sand the post and the base, then join them with glue and flathead wood screws.

Grind a point on the steel pivot rod. To do this, mount the pivot rod in the chuck of a hand-held power drill. Turn on the drill and hold the exposed end of the rod at a 45-degree angle to a running disc sander. (The drill must rotate in the *opposite direction* from the disc sander.) Press the rod lightly against the disc until the end is ground to a point. Insert the pivot rod in the hole in the top of the post, pointed end up.

6 Check the operation of the wind wheel and wind vane. Place a flat washer over the pivot rod. Then place the wind vane assembly over the pivot (atop the washer) and the wind wheel assembly on top of the pivot. Spin the wind wheel by hand to make sure the paddles don't hit any part of the wind vane assembly. If they do, raise the wind wheel slightly by removing the pivot from the post and inserting a short length of ¼-inch dowel into the pivot hole. When you're satisfied the wheel and the wind vane operate properly, glue the pivot rod in the post with epoxy.

7 Attach the figures and balance the wheel. Cut two ⅝-inch-long pieces of wire for the front legs of the mouse, two ¾-inch-long pieces for the back legs, and a 1-inch-long piece for the tail. Secure the wires in the ³/₃₂-inch-diameter holes in the mouse body with epoxy cement. Glue the dowels in the figures, then mount the figures on the wind wheel assembly. Once the figures are attached, the wheel will be unbalanced, since the woman and dog figures are larger and heavier than the other two. It will be slightly angled toward the woman, causing it to bind on the pivot.

Bring the wheel back into balance using fender washers as counterweights. Stack up washers, one at a time, on the opposite side of the wheel from the woman, near the head of the cat. Keep adding washers until the wheel just begins to angle toward the cat. Remove one washer, then attach the stack to the underside of the wheel (under the same spot where you stacked them) with a roundhead wood screw. Once the wheel is balanced, it will spin more easily.

You may also want to balance the wind vane assembly so it turns more freely. Because the wind vane protrudes farther from the pivot than the wind shield, the assembly will be slightly angled toward the vane. Stack washers on the wind shield brace until the assembly balances, then attach the washers to the underside of the brace.

8 Paint the whirligig. Do any necessary touchup sanding, then paint the features of the figures, wind wheel, wind shield, and wind vane. Be sure to paint *all* exposed wood surfaces, including the underside of the wheel. Use artist's acrylic paints — these stand up well to weather and sunlight. They are available at most paint stores and graphic supply stores. For extra protection, coat the painted surfaces with clear exterior water-based varnish.

INDEX

Note: Page references in *italic* indicate photographs or illustrations.
Boldface references indicate charts or tables.

WOODWORKING GLOSSARY

TENON DETAIL
CHEEK
SHOULDER

MORTISE
TENON

NOTCH
LAP JOINT

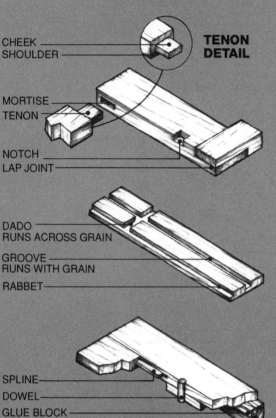

DADO
RUNS ACROSS GRAIN

GROOVE
RUNS WITH GRAIN

RABBET

SPLINE
DOWEL
GLUE BLOCK

BASIC JOINERY

FINGERS

FINGER JOINT

PIN

TAIL

DOVETAIL JOINT

BLIND DADO

BLIND RABBET

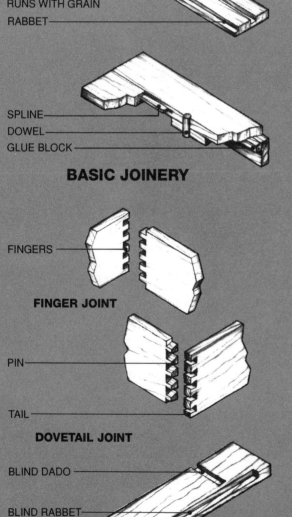

SPECIAL JOINERY

STRAIGHT

TAPERED

CABRIOLE

COMMON SHAPES

CROSSCUT
MITER
RIP
BEVEL

BASIC SAW CUTS

COUNTERBORE
COUNTERSINK
PILOT HOLE

SCREW HOLE
STOPPED HOLE
THRU HOLE

HOLES

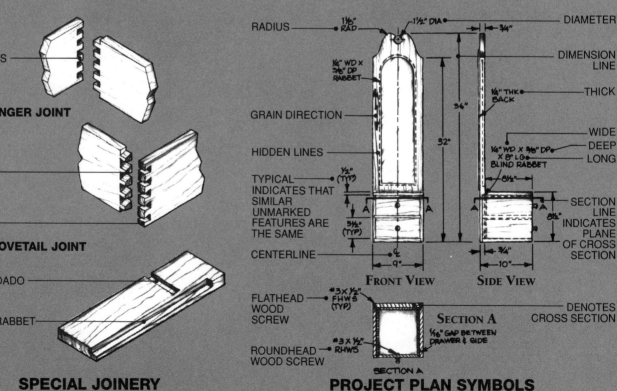

RADIUS
1½" RAD
1½" DIA
¾"
DIAMETER

¼" WD X
⅜" DP
RABBET

DIMENSION
LINE

¼" THK
BACK

THICK

36"

32"

GRAIN DIRECTION

HIDDEN LINES

¼" WD X ⅜" DP
X 8" LG
BLIND RABBET

WIDE
DEEP
LONG

TYPICAL
INDICATES THAT
SIMILAR
UNMARKED
FEATURES ARE
THE SAME

½"
(TYP)

3½"
(TYP)

8½"

8½"

SECTION
LINE
INDICATES
PLANE
OF CROSS
SECTION

CENTERLINE

¢

9"

¾"

10"

FRONT VIEW   **SIDE VIEW**

FLATHEAD
WOOD
SCREW

#3 X ½"
FHWS
(TYP)

ROUNDHEAD
WOOD SCREW

#3 X ½"
RHWS

SECTION A

1/16" GAP BETWEEN
DRAWER & SIDE

DENOTES
CROSS SECTION

SECTION A

PROJECT PLAN SYMBOLS